Socrates and Legal Obligation

Socrates and Legal Obligation

R. E. Allen

Department of Philosophy and Classics
Northwestern University

University of Minnesota Press • Minneapolis

Copyright © 1980 by the University of Minnesota.
All rights reserved.
Published by the University of Minnesota Press,
2037 University Avenue Southeast,
Minneapolis MN 55414
Printed in the United States of America.

Library of Congress Cataloging in Publication Data

Allen, Reginald E.   1931-
    Socrates and legal obligation.
    Includes the author's translations of Plato's Apology
and Crito.
    Bibliography: p.
    Includes index.
    1. Plato. Apologia. 2. Plato. Crito.
3. Socrates. 4. Law—Philosophy. I. Plato. Apologia.
English. 1980. II. Plato. Crito. English. 1980.
III. Title.
B365.A95   184   80-18193
ISBN 0-8166-0962-4
ISBN 0-8166-0965-9 (pbk.)

The University of Minnesota
is an equal-opportuntity
educator and employer.

For Ruth and Elisabeth

Although I cannot say that I am utterly untrained
in those rules which best rhetoricians have given
or unacquainted with those examples which the prime
authors of eloquence have written in any learned
tongue, yet true eloquence I find to be none but
the serious and hearty love of truth; and that
whose mind is soever fully possessed with a desire
to know good things, and with the dearest charity to
infuse the knowledge of them into others, when such
should speak, his words (by what I can express) like
so many nimble and airy servitors trip about him at
command, and in well-ordered files, as he would
wish, fall aptly into their places.

John Milton, Apology

Introduction

The association between Plato's *Crito* and *Apology* is close and natural. They were anciently grouped by Thrasyllus with the *Euthyphro* and *Phaedo* as members of a single tetralogy, the first, for the reason that they bear on the events of Socrates' trial and death. The scene of the *Euthyphro* is the Porch of the King Archon, where Socrates has come to answer in preliminary hearing the charges brought against him by Meletus; the *Apology* presents Socrates' courtroom defense and condemnation; the *Crito*, his refusal to escape the death sentence a few days before it was to be executed; the *Phaedo*, his last hours and death, and promise of immortality. This order has to do with the sequence of events described, not with the chronology of description. On stylistic grounds, the *Phaedo* must be classified as a middle dialogue, written well after its tetralogical companions. But there is no compelling reason, stylistic or otherwise, to suppose that the *Crito* was written after rather than before the *Apology*,[1] or for that matter the *Euthyphro*. It is sufficient to observe that they are works of Plato's early period, probably written between 399 and 387 B.C., when Plato was in his thirties.

What follows is not meant as a commentary, which Burnet has admirably provided. My aim has been to help the reader understand certain elements in the *Apology* and *Crito* which have often proved obscure, and the comment is relatively more full in dealing with the

Crito than the *Apology* because of the greater complexity of the jurisprudential issues there raised. The interpretation of the *Apology* involves questions of literature, philosophy, and comparative law
which have not, in general, been asked; the reasons for the peculiar
kind of defense Socrates made at his trial have passed largely unrecog-
nized, as has the complex irony which that defense displays, and the
legal quality of the conviction. If this is reason enough for fresh comment on the *Apology*, the subtle and cogent argument of the *Crito*
provides better reason still: for the *Crito* has not been well understood even by those professionally concerned to interpret it, with the
result that one of the great masterpieces of legal philosophy in western literature has been made to seem philosophically trivial. If the
account which follows succeeds in making the *Apology* better understood, and helps restore the *Crito* to its rightful place as a classic
statement of the grounds of legal obligation, it will have served its
purpose.

Portions of the account have appeared elsewhere. The first chapter,
"Irony and Rhetoric in Plato's *Apology*," was the Cowling Lecture in
Philosophy for 1977 at Carleton College, where such colleagues and
friends as David and Mary Alice Sipfle, Fred and Judy Stoutland of
St. Olaf's, and Gary and Andrea Iseminger, added zest for teaching
and hospitality to the slow glories of a Minnesota spring. A draft of
the lecture in cruder form had previously been read to the classics
departments at Princeton and Pittsburgh; it has since been published
in *Paideia*. The chapter on legality, in much revised form, was first
read in 1974 before the Faculty of Law, University of Toronto, as
part of a series of seminars sponsored by the Canadian Commission
on Law Reform; it was afterward published in *Courts and Trials*,
edited by Dean M. L. Friedland and presented to The Right Honorable
Borah Laskin, Chief Justice of Canada. The analysis of the *Crito* offered here was first presented in outline form in a paper entitled
"Law and Justice in Plato's *Crito*," read as part of a symposium of
the American Philosophical Association in 1971 given with Charles
Kahn and G. E. L. Owen, and printed in the *Journal of Philosophy*
for 1972. It remains to say that it is unlikely that the present form
of this work would be as it is had it not been for Mrs. Clare Kirk-
patrick, R.N., Nurse Clinician, who, out of sheer humanity, exhibited
in practical application the truth of the Socratic theorem that the virtues are one, and especially the virtues of courage and wisdom.

My debts are many and various. Jerome Hall first directed my attention to many of the jurisprudential problems here discussed. Har-
old Cherniss was responsible for many improvements, and lent loyal

support. John Swan and Ernest Weinrib, in a series of seminars on jurisprudence in the Faculty of Law, University of Toronto, taught me more philosophy than I would otherwise have known. Dean Eugene V. Rostow took time from a busy schedule to criticize my interpretation of the *Crito* in terms of his own valuable analysis in "The Rightful Limits of Freedom."[2] The account that follows has also benefitted in many ways, indirect but certain, from the hospitality and instruction of The Honorable Edwin H. Stier, Director of the Division of Criminal Justice of the State of New Jersey, and of William F. Bolan, Jr., now Chief of the Educational and Legislative Services Section, who introduced me to the law in action at a level of highest professionalism, and confirmed my belief that many of the issues here discussed in terms of the past belong to the living present. It goes without saying that the mistakes which remain philosophical, philological, historical, and legal—are my own.

Translations of the *Apology* and *Crito* have been included, not because the world is groaning for them—they have been well translated already—but as an aid to the reader and a control on interpretation. Translation and comment alike are much indebted to Burnet, whose scholarship does not wear out.

Contents

Socrates and Legal Obligation

The Apology

Irony and Rhetoric
in Plato's *Apology*

In the year 399 B.C., in Athens, Socrates, son of Sophroniscus, of the deme Alopece, aged seventy, was brought to trial on a writ of impiety, a *graphe asebeias*. He was found guilty and condemned to death. The exact indictment, or, more accurately perhaps, sworn information, has been preserved by Diogenes Laertius on the authority of the scholar Favorinus, who searched the Athenian archives and found it there:

This indictment and affidavit is sworn by Meletus, the son of Meletus of Pitthos, against Socrates, the son of Sophroniscus of Alopece: Socrates is guilty of refusing to recognize the gods recognized by the state, and of introducing other new divinities. He is also guilty of corrupting the youth. The penalty demanded is death.[1]

There were, then, three counts: refusing to acknowledge the gods acknowledged by the City; introducing new (or strange, *kaina*) divinities; and corrupting the youth.

It was, of course, a celebrated case, and for years afterward controversy swirled around the verdict. Unlike most controversies, however, this one produced great literature—specifically, Plato's *Apology*. The *Apology* is not a dialogue but a speech, a speech of such force and directness that at one level it cannot be misunderstood. Yet despite its surface simplicity, it is a complex document, and contains

3

several levels of irony in the depths of its complexity. Irony, indeed, attaches to its very name. An *apologia* is a defense. But the *Apology* is something other than a defense, as that term is generally understood.

The Silence of Socrates

There is a Hellenistic tradition, preserved by the rhetorician Libanius[2] and Maximus of Tyre, that Socrates at his trial stood mute or at least had as good as nothing to say in his own behalf. The tradition is late, and 'the Silence of Socrates' might easily be dismissed—if it were not for the fact that it is supported by and almost certainly derived from Plato's *Gorgias*.

Callicles in the *Gorgias* attacks philosophy and condemns it as useless—a charming thing to pursue while young, if done in moderation, but the ruin of a man if pursued too intensely or too long. His advice to Socrates issues in a prediction:

If someone were to take you or anyone like you and drag you off to jail, accusing you of guilt when you had done no wrong, you know perfectly well that you wouldn't know what to do. You would gape with dizziness, and you wouldn't have a word to say. And once brought to court, though your accuser was ever so contemptible a knave, if he chose to exact the death penalty, you would die. [*Gorgias* 486a-b]

Socrates himself later repeats the prediction. He is led to claim at the conclusion of his discussion with Callicles that he is the only true statesman in Athens, and to foresee his own death. Put on trial, he will have nothing to say in his own defense: "I shall be like a doctor tried before a jury of children on charges brought by a pastry-cook." The doctor, whose healing ministrations consist in cutting and burning and vile-tasting doses, would have nothing to say in his own behalf.

And I know if I were brought into court, it would be the same with me. . . . If someone accuses me of corrupting the youth by reducing them to perplexity, or doing ill to their elders with sharp and pointed speech, in public or private, I won't be able to tell the truth, which is that, "I say these things rightly, Gentlemen and judges, and do so for your benefit"—nor will I be able to say anything else. The result will no doubt be that I'll take what comes. [*Gorgias* 522b]

This is a strong variation on a theme which recurs in many dialogues: the helplessness of the philosopher in a court of law. He will appear ridiculous to the multitude, and even mad. So far, at least, Callicles was right.

In the *Apology*, of course, Socrates has a great deal to say, and says it with high art. Yet the *Gorgias* passage, so far from contradicting the *Apology*, is meant as a comment on it. As Professor Dodds remarks, "The pastrycook's speech is a witty parody of the complaints brought against Socrates at his trial."[3] It may be added that the speech is followed by a passage which recapitulates the main theme of the *Apology*: that the only genuine evil is the evil of wickedness, that for the good man there is no evil in death, as there is none in life. The myth which concludes the *Gorgias* provides that theme with an eschatology.

Rhetoric in the *Apology*

Socrates cannot speak in his own defense, yet the *Gorgias* is a comment on the *Apology*. This is incongruous, and the incongruity is repeated within the body of the *Apology* itself.

The *Apology* falls into three main parts: Socrates' speech of defense (17a-35d); the speech of the counterpenalty, after conviction (35e-38b); and an epilogue, addressed respectively to those who voted for and against condemnation (38c-42a). It is the first and longest of these, the speech of defense, which is here in view.

The problem with that speech, simply stated, is that it seems to bear the mark of falsehood on its face. In the introduction to it (18a-19a), Socrates denies that he has any skill in speaking, unless that means ability to speak the truth. He asks his judges to overlook the fact that he will make his defense with the same *logoi*—the word could mean 'arguments', but in context would have been taken by his audience to mean 'words'—which he has been accustomed to use in the marketplace. He remarks on his advanced age, on the fact that he has not previously been brought to trial, and on his unfamiliarity with the ways of the law courts. As Riddell long ago pointed out,[4] all of this can be paralleled point by point in other speeches which have come down to us by Lysias, Isocrates, and Aeschines. The man who cannot make a speech is providing a textbook example of a forensic exordium.

The exordium is not only rhetorical. It is, as Burnet pointed out,[5] a rhetorical parody of rhetoric. The diction is far removed from the marketplace: it is periodic, and marked by the neatly balanced antitheses characteristic of Greek rhetorical style.[6] As with diction, so with structure. The speech, having begun with a proper Exordium, proceeds to a Prothesis, a statement of the case and plan of the plea (18a-19a); it then offers a Refutation (19a-28a), directed first against the Old Accusers who have raised prejudice against Socrates (19a-24b), and then to the actual charges brought by Meletus with the support of Anytus and Lycon (24b-28a); there follows a Digression (28a-34b), normally used to win the audience to the speaker's side, here used to describe Socrates' peculiar mission to Athens; the speech then closes with a well-marked Peroration (34b-35d). As Dyer and Seymour remark, "All the laws of oratorical art are here carefully observed, though the usual practices of oratory are sharply criticised. The five natural heads of the argument are unmistakable."[7]

So Socrates makes a speech and, as it happens, we have a remarkable piece of contemporary evidence to show how highly that speech was regarded. Isocrates, a young man at the time of the trial, later founded a school of rhetoric in Athens which competed with the Academy. At the end of his long life, he wrote a kind of *apologia pro sua vita*, the *Antidosis*. He there adopts the fiction of a capital charge brought against him by an informer, and constructs a set-piece courtroom defense. At point after point, he implicitly compares himself to Socrates, and studiously echoes the speech of the *Apology*.[8] From a self-acknowledged master of rhetoric, a tribute: the *Apology* was regarded in its own time as a paradigm of rhetorical art.

This, then, is the first level of irony in Socrates' speech of defense. Irony, pitched at its lowest, is saying less than you think, and sometimes the opposite of what you mean. It looks mightily like dishonesty. The first level of irony in the *Apology* presents the apparent falsehood: Socrates disclaims ability to make a speech, and proceeds to make so able a speech that it is a masterpiece of rhetoric.

Rhetorical Incongruity

But the *Apology* is a highly peculiar masterpiece. Socrates constructs an engine of rhetoric according to a well-marked plan. But engines have a function, and the function of forensic rhetoric is to win conviction if prosecuting and acquittal if accused. The engine Socrates constructs does not work this way at all. So far from aiming at acquittal, the speech avowedly aims at telling the truth in accordance with justice even if the truth leads to conviction. So far from attempting to prove the charges in the indictment false, it does not so much as deny them. There is, then, gross incongruity between the form of the speech and its function: in diction and structure a superb example of forensic rhetoric, it is not in method and aim rhetorical, in the ordinary sense, at all.

Indeed, Socrates does not deny the charges against him. He meets the charge of irreligion by cross-examining Meletus, his accuser, and trapping him in inconsistency. Meletus is incautious enough to assert that Socrates acknowledges no gods, that he is a complete atheist, after having sworn in his indictment that Socrates had introduced new divinities. Socrates merely shows that since divinities are either gods or children of gods, acknowledgment of divinities implies acknowledgment of gods (26b-27e). He later denies atheism in stated terms (35d); but he does not deny, presumably for the reason given in the *Euthyphro* (6a-b; cf. 5a-b), namely, that he finds it difficult to accept the traditional stories of the gods' hatred and enmity toward each other, the charge of not acknowledging the gods the City acknowledges. Nor does he anywhere deny the charge of introducing strange divinities; he only explains the charge by referring it to his accustomed Sign, which he explicitly describes as godlike and divine. (31d; cf. *Euthyphro* 36). Again, he nowhere denies corrupting the youth. He argues against Meletus that either he does not corrupt them or he corrupts them unintentionally (25d-26a)—but this is not to deny that he corrupts them. He offers witnesses who will testify on the point in his behalf, and he suggests that Meletus call them (33d-34b). He denies that he corrupts by teaching, on the ground that he has never taught nor taken money for it; but he admits that it is open to any man to hear what he has to say (33a-b). The closest he comes to denying the charge of corrupting the youth is to describe his peculiar mission to Athens—that of turning men to the pursuit of virtue at the behest of the God at Delphi—and to add, "*If* in saying these things I corrupt the youth, that would be harm indeed" (30a-b; cf. *Euthyphro* 2c-3a). Finally, he nowhere denies the charge of impiety, though he suggests a type of defense, expected and unoffered, which would have made him guilty of it (35c-d).

So Socrates, in his speech of defense, does not so much as deny the charges formally lodged against him and on which he is being tried.

This, then, is the second level of irony in the *Apology*. The man who cannot give a speech gives a speech. The speech he gives suggests he cannot give a speech. On trial for his life, in a circumstance which calls for all the arts of forensic rhetoric, he offers rhetoric which is not forensic.

Counter-Rhetoric

Socrates' speech, indeed, might easily be construed as a kind of counter-rhetoric.

Consider the mere fact that, in diction and structure, Socrates' speech is rhetorical. The bulk of his Refutation is directed, not toward

Meletus and the formal indictment, but toward the prejudice raised against him by the Old Accusers, especially Aristophanes, for the reason that, as Socrates himself suggests, he was confused in the popular mind with the Sophists. Aristophanes had portrayed him in the *Clouds* as a man who inquired into things in the heavens and beneath the earth, and made the weaker argument stronger; as Socrates remarks, "The men who spread that report are my dangerous accusers; for their hearers believe that those who inquire into such things acknowledge no gods" (18c). The charge of making the weaker argument stronger— Wrong Logic triumphs over Right Logic in the *Clouds*—was particularly damaging, carrying with it the implication of pernicious skepticism, associated with Sophistry.[9] The Sophists' stock in trade was rhetoric and, given that Socrates was popularly identified with them, and that this was a serious matter of complaint, true rhetoric would require that he abstain from anything that even looked like rhetoric. Had he chosen to conduct his defense in the plain speech he seemed to have promised, he would have done much to allay the prejudice against him; even as it was, the vote was very close (36a). Instead, he disclaims ability to speak in the course of a masterful speech, before an audience thoroughly familiar with the uses of political and forensic oratory. His hearers would not have found the apparent attempt at deception amusing. Irony, *eironeia*, was no virtue, but a defect of character, as Theophrastus' portrait of the Ironical Man in the *Characters* makes clear: it was an attribute typically associated with foxes —and with Socrates (38a; cf. *Republic* I 337a, *Symposium* 216e). Thus, though Socrates denies point by point the general portrait offered of him in the *Clouds*, his use of rhetoric suggests sophistry, and the very skill of his use confirms the suggestion. His substantive claims, though true, are made to seem false by the manner in which they are issued. In circumstances which call for appearing as an ordinary, domesticated farmyard fowl, he has given himself the character of the fox.

As Aristotle remarks, one rule of rhetoric is to make your character look right. This Socrates does not do. Another rule is to put your audience in the right frame of mind:

When people are feeling friendly and placable, they think one sort of thing; when they are feeling angry and hostile, they think either something totally different or the same thing with a different intensity: when they feel friendly to the man who comes before them for judgment, they regard him as having done little wrong, if any; when they feel hostile, they take the opposite view.[10]

Clearly, if you mean to persuade, it is best not to offend, and the advice becomes more urgent if you are pleading a cause before five hundred dicasts who will function both as jurors and judges, finding law as well as fact, and who will be moved, humanly, quite as much by their emotions as their intellect.

Socrates does little enough to make his jurors feel 'friendly and placable'. The manner in which he deals with the counterpenalty stands as a vivid symbol of the speech of defense itself. He has been found guilty. Meletus has proposed death. Socrates must suggest an alternate penalty, and between those two penalties the court by law must choose—no splitting the difference. At this of all points, Socrates suggests that if penalty is to be assessed according to desert, his penalty should be public subsistence in the Prytaneum in the manner of an Olympic victor. The same tone is a constant undercurrent in his speech of defense. He disclaims clever speaking before an audience well-familiar with its devices, and he uses clever speech. He uses rhetoric to deny sophistry. On trial for impiety, he politely explains that the conduct which brought him to that court was prompted by obedience to God. Before a jury holding power of life and death, he says that he will not give over his service to the God, no manner what their decision: "If, as I say, you were to dismiss me on the condition that I cease to pursue philosophy, I would reply that I hold you in friendship and esteem, Gentlemen of Athens, but I shall obey the God rather than you, and while I have breath and am able, I shall not cease to pursue wisdom and to exhort you" (29d). In the circumstances, this appears to be something very close to outright defiance. After remarking that his habit of cross-questioning people—itself associated with sophistry and making the weaker argument stronger—has been a source not only of prejudice but of hatred against him, he then gives a public specimen of it in his cross-examination of Meletus; the results are devastating, but, in the circumstances, they tell against Socrates himself. He attacks politicians, poets, and craftsmen for claiming knowledge of things of which they are ignorant before a jury of five hundred men and a large and restless audience, most of whom had served in some political office, most of whom were craftsmen, and most of whom regarded poets as sources of moral and religious instruction. Socrates is here doing something more than suggesting to his judges that they are a group of ignorant men. He is punching an exposed political nerve. He is telling a jury of democrats, who have sore and vivid recollections of oligarchical persecution under the Thirty Tyrants, and genuine fear for the stability of their reconstitued

Democracy, that they and their leadership are grossly and radically ignorant, if not morally bankrupt. He goes so far, indeed, as to suggest that it is impossible for a decent man to play an active part in political life and survive (31e-32a). He is speaking to a large group of survivors.

Socrates, in short, challenges the basic piety on which government by the Many rested—and his habit of so doing was a principal reason for the charge that he corrupted the youth. It is beside the point that he would have challenged with equal effect the pieties of government by the few.

All this, and more, is in Socrates' speech of defense. It is magnificent. But if rhetoric is the faculty of observing, in each case, the available means of persuasion,[11] it is not rhetoric. Disclaiming clever speech, Socrates gives a speech which seems too clever by half, and is not half clever enough. He offers rhetoric which seems very like the opposite of rhetoric.

Two Concepts of Rhetoric

I have already suggested that the connection between the *Gorgias* and the *Apology* is intimate. To understand more fully how this is so, it is helpful to realize that the *Gorgias* puts forward not one but two concepts of rhetoric.

In its usual acceptation, rhetoric is the power of persuasion, indifferent to truth. So it is that Gorgias, after several false starts, is led to define it as "the ability to persuade with words—in law courts, in Council and Assembly, in civic gatherings of any kind" (452e). The persuasion involved has primarily to do with what is just and unjust (454b), but it is irrational, in that it is based, not on knowledge derived from instruction, but on belief without knowledge: Socrates sums things up thus:

> Rhetoric, it seems, produces persuasion about right and wrong which rests on belief without instruction. So the orator does not instruct courts and other crowds about right and wrong: he merely persuades. For after all, it would hardly be possible to instruct a large crowd in a short time about matters of such importance. [455a; cf. *Apology* 19a, 24a]

Rhetoric is, in fact, a kind of trick. The orator has no need to know the actual truth of things, for his aim is persuasion, which enables him to appear to the ignorant to know more than those who have knowledge (459c).

This is why, in conversation with Polus, Socrates denies that rhetoric is an art at all; for art implies knowledge, and rhetoric lacks knowledge and cannot render an account: it is *alogon*, as lacking a *logos*. It is a mere knack, the intellectual counterpart of pastry cooking, a species of *kolakeia* – 'flattery', though the word has baser connotations – aimed at gratification and pleasure, and indifferent to truth. Though often mistaken for statesmanship, it is a mere image or counterfeit of statesmanship. It stands to the art of the statesman as pastry-cooking stands to medicine, and so far from being a noble thing, as Polus has claimed, it is base (see esp. 464b-465a). The same point is put succinctly and forcefully by Socrates in the *Phaedrus* (260c):

When a rhetorician ignorant of good and evil tries to persuade a city similarly circumstanced, not by praising the shadow of an ass as if it were a horse, but by praising evil as if it were good, and having studied the beliefs of the multitude, persuades them to do what is evil instead of good, what harvest do you think his rhetoric will reap from the seeds he has sown?

This sort of rhetoric Socrates condemns as a mere artless knack, an *atechnos tribē*. As the point is put in the *Gorgias*, "A real art of speaking which does not lay hold of truth does not exist and never will" (*Gorgias* 260e).

This talk of 'rhetoric' may seem pleasantly archaic to the contemporary reader, and quite irrelevant to today's business. The appearance will be removed if he bethinks himself of the content of most of the political discourse he hears, or the works of the advertising agency. He will then better understand what is meant by *kolakeia*, and a knack without a *logos*.

But the *Gorgias*, like the *Phaedrus* (see *Phaedrus* 269e ff.), carries matters further. In argument with Callicles, Socrates envisages another sort of rhetoric: a philosophical rhetoric aimed at truth and excellence of soul, whether it gives pleasure or pain to the hearers, an *art* of rhetoric, based on knowledge, whose object is to produce justice and that order of soul associated with lawfulness and law. The practitioner of this kind of rhetoric stands to the soul as the physician stands to the body; he is not an image of the statesman, but the statesman himself. When he speaks, he does not speak at random but, like a craftsman, organizes his materials with a view to his single aim (503-e; cf. *Phaedrus* 26c-d, *Crito* 47c-e). A palmary example of this sort of rhetoric is the speech of the Laws of Athens in the *Crito* (50a-54d); it may be compared to the aimless order of the rhetoric in Crito's plea to Socrates to escape (45a-46a), which, like the epitaph of Midas the Phrygian, lacks both head and foot (cf. *Phaedrus* 263 c-d).

There are, then, two concepts of rhetoric in the *Gorgias*: base rhetoric, aiming at gratification and pleasure, and indifferent to truth or the good of the soul; and philosophical rhetoric, aiming at truth and the good of the soul, and indifferent to gratification and pleasure.

This association between philosophical rhetoric and the art of the statesman, on the ground that both possess knowledge and an art directed toward the good of the soul, is the basis of the astonishing claim, from a man who held public office only once in his life, and then as it appears by sortition, that Socrates is the one true statesman in Athens. Not surprisingly, when put on his trial, he was mistaken for something else. In a dialogue written many years after the *Gorgias* and *Apology*, an Eleatic Stranger, searching for the Sophist, stumbles across a class of men who purify the soul from deceit; they are not Sophists, though they have some resemblance to them. But then, as the Stranger remarks, "So has the dog to the wolf—the fiercest of animals to the tamest. But a cautious man should above all be on his guard against resemblances; they are a very slippery sort of thing" (Sophist 231a, trans. Comford). As the *Phaedrus* (262a-c) makes clear, you can deal with resemblances only if you understand the nature of things: dogs and wolves are easily mistaken at a distance. In the *Apology*, Socrates practices an art of persuasion founded on truth, and ignorance, not surprisingly, mistakes it for a form of base rhetoric—though no doubt a queer one. The philosopher is taken for the Sophist, the dog for the wolf.

Irony and Rhetoric

The two concepts of rhetoric in the *Gorgias* answer to the two levels of irony in the *Apology*. The rhetoric to which Socrates in the *Apology* adheres is a rhetoric directed not at persuasion but at truth (35b-d; cf. 17b, 38d-39a): to the degree that his speech required the kind of persuasion that only flattery could produce, to the degree that it required forensic rhetoric, Socrates gave no speech at all. Socrates is the doctor before a jury of children. He offers philosophical rhetoric where he was expected to offer forensic rhetoric, with its attendant *kolakeia*; he cannot offer the latter because he is a philosopher, not a Sophist. Thus it is that, tried on a charge of impiety, he is prevented by concern for piety from putting forward the expected defense (35c-d). Thus it is that, found guilty and condemned, he tells those who voted for his conviction that he has not been found guilty for lack of words to convince them, had he chosen to use them, but for lack of bold shamelessness in saying the things they would have found it most pleasant to hear—"weeping and wailing, saying and doing a multitude of things I hold to be unworthy, but things of a sort you are accustomed to hear from others (38d-e; cf. 34b-35a). Philosophical rhetoric can accomplish the aim of forensic rhetoric only *per accidens*, if at all; in Socrates' case, it failed *per accidens* precisely because it did not fail of its own aim.

Big Talk

This explanation answers an ancient question which puzzled Xenophon: Why did not Socrates defend himself to better effect? Xenophon began his own *Apology of Socrates* with an attempt at an answer:

> It seems to me fitting to hand down to memory, furthermore, how Socrates, on being indicted, deliberated on his defense and on his end. It is true that others have written about this, and that all of them have reproduced the loftiness of his words (*megalegoria*)—a fact which proves that his utterance really was of the character intimated;—but they have not shown clearly that he had now come to the conclusion that for him death was more to be desired than life; and hence his lofty utterance appears rather ill-considered. [para. 1, trans. Todd]

Megalegoria means more than 'loftiness of words'. It means 'big talk', and implies arrogance. If Socrates spoke as Plato represents him, Xenophon found his *megalegoria* unexplained.[12]

Xenophon's explanation of the 'loftiness' is that Socrates' Sign opposed preparation of a defense,[13] and that Socrates inferred from this that the God thought it better for him to die now and so be spared the evils of old age. This merely picks up a minor theme at the end of Plato's *Apology*: "What has now come did not come of its own initiative: it is clear that to die now and be released from my concerns is better for me. That is why the Sign did not turn me back" (41d). Xenophon himself is something less than consistent in his account, since he goes on to make Socrates provide a point by point refutation of the charges, while yet maintaining that the 'loftiness' is aimed at obtaining conviction (to the contrary, see Plato, *Apology* 34d). Socrates, so far from attempting to gain acquittal, was actively courting condemnation—suicide by judicial process, one of the rarer forms of suicide by blunt instrument.

As we have seen, the true explanation lies elsewhere. Socrates' aim was to gain neither conviction nor acquittal, but to tell the truth in accordance with justice, let the chips fall where they may. Acquittal could only have been obtained by a defense which would have amounted to abject pandering, *kolakeia*, a defense which, because it corrupted the true function of a judge, Socrates himself declares to be impious, as causing judges to forswear themselves (35d).

The 'Silence of Socrates' is not silence, but speech based on truth, and fatal in the circumstances. Socrates' character, in the *Apology*, is of a piece with his character in the *Euthyphro* and other early dialogues of search. Because he knew himself to be ignorant in matters which appeared obvious to men who thought themselves wise, he seemed sly and dishonest: irony, sometimes, is in the eye of the beholder. But his ignorance was real, not feigned, and it issued in a form of inquiry which involved *elenchus*, refutation. The merit of *elenchus* was to purge the false conceit of knowledge; but if it thereby chastened, it also stirred many men to wrath, and their anger was kindled higher by the appearance of Wrong Logic and deceit. Socrates had no wish to be hated. His service to the God caused him to be hated, and he perceived the fact with grief and pain. But he still maintained the soldier's station in which the God had placed him. Brought into court and compelled to abandon his customary form of inquiry by question and answer, he aimed at truth, so far as he could tell it, about his own character and the nature of his mission to Athens. Because he was, after all, an ignorant man, he adopted the received form appropriate to the occasion, the form of forensic rhetoric without its content, and by its use proclaimed his ignorance to those who thought themselves wise. The result appeared to be an astonishing arrogance. His was not the guarded truth of a defendant on trial for his life; it appeared, in fact, very like the truth of a prophet in calm wrath. But Socrates was carrying on philosophy by other means. If he was hated for telling the truth, it was not because he was indifferent to the hate, but because he was not indifferent to the truth. His speech is not an exhibition of arrogance, but of service to the God and his own mission, and of that courage, allied to wisdom, which consists in knowing when and when not to be afraid.

This is why Socrates not only did not, but could not, answer the charges against him. Whatever else we may think of Meletus, and Anytus and Lycon, his accusers, they had seen deeply enough into the character of the man they pursued to draw up an indictment distinguished by its lawyerly cunning, an indictment Socrates could no more have answered than a child. Socrates, wiser than other men only in knowing that he did not know, could not with knowledge deny the charges against him. He was indicted on a writ of impiety. But in order to know whether or not his conduct had been impious, it was necessary first to know what piety is, its essential idea or nature; he had sought to learn in the *Euthyphro* (6d-e; cf. 5a-b, 15e), in order to prepare for the trial, and had failed. Does impiety lie for urging men to pursue virtue—and convicting them of ignorance? That question cannot be answered with knowledge, truth in accordance with justice, by a man who knows himself to be ignorant of what piety is.

As with the writ, so with the counts. A man who does not know what virtue is (*Meno* 71b-c, and passim) can deny that he intentionally corrupts the youth; but he cannot deny that he corrupts them, since knowledge of vice implies knowledge of its opposite, and he does not know what virtue is. He can deny that he corrupts by teaching if in fact he has never taught but only questioned. But he cannot deny that he corrupts by introducing strange divinities and not acknowledging old ones if he is himself ignorant, not only in matters of virtue, but of religion (26c, *Euthyphro* 3b). Does one or does one not acknowledge the gods the City acknowledges, if one doubts that certain of the terrible stories told about them, and embroidered on the Robe carried to the Acropolis at the Greater Panathenaea, are true (cf. *Euthyphro* 6a-b)? Does one corrupt the youth by expressing those doubts? Can one or can one not deny the introduction of strange divinities, given the presence of an accustomed Sign believed to be divine? Does one corrupt the youth by mentioning the Sign? To deny such charges on the basis of knowledge—on the basis of truth in accordance with justice—one must first understand what they mean; that understanding requires inquiry into precisely the things of which Socrates knew himself to be ignorant—for example, the real nature of virtue, the real nature of piety. The appropriate inquiry would take more time than was offered by a law court, speaking against a water clock. It is not too much to say, indeed, that a lifetime had already proved too short. The doctor, put on trial before a jury of children on charges brought by a clever pastry cook, has nothing to say.

So the two levels of irony in the *Apology* mesh. The man who cannot give a speech gives a speech. The speech he gives proves that he cannot give a speech. The two levels are so related as to turn apparent falsehood into literal truth.

This is not to say that Socrates does not reply to Meletus. If Socrates does not know what piety and impiety are, he knows at least this much, namely, that Meletus does not know either. If he knows that he cannot answer the charges "in truth according to justice," he also knows—and, by his cross-examination and refutation of Meletus, proves—that his accusers could not "in truth according to justice" bring them against him. He departs convicted by the Athenians of impiety, and sentenced to death. They depart convicted by the truth of villainy and injustice, and will abide their penalty (39b; cf. 36d). This is not a defense against the charges, but in the nature of a counterclaim.

One may take matters a step further. By his use of rhetoric without forensic content, Socrates does not state but shows the difference between base rhetoric and philosophical rhetoric, and also shows that the difference is not a matter of form. The verdict of the Athenians indicates that, as Meletus and those around him do not know what piety and impiety are, so the Athenians do not know what sophistry is, or what it means for the stronger argument to be strong. Standing at a distance from reality, they cannot tell a dog from a wolf. What is shown is not said, and cannot be said except to those who have learned to see and therefore do not need to hear it.

There is indeed a silence of Socrates. It exists, not only in the *Apology*, but in every early dialogue in which he inquires by refutation. It testifies, perhaps, that only those who care most about words have most fully learned their seriousness and their ultimate uselessness, and learned too, on occasion, like Prospero, to summon a solemn music and, deeper than did ever plummet sound, drown their book.

The Historical Background of the Charges

The author of the *Seventh Epistle*, writing some forty years or more after the trial, described Socrates as the best and most righteous man of his time, and dismissed the charge of impiety as one which he least of all men deserved. Whether or not those are Plato's own words, they most certainly represent Plato's own views (see *Phaedo* 118a) and those of many other Athenians. Yet Socrates died a condemned criminal.

Impiety, no doubt, was a serious matter. A sign of this is that it was prosecuted by *graphē* or writ of public indictment, as technically even murder was not, because it directly affected the welfare and safety of the City as a whole. As Euthyphro puts it, "Piety preserves both families and cities and keeps them safe. The opposite of what is acceptable to the gods is impious, and impiety overturns and destroys all things" (14b). To leave impiety unpunished was to invite divine retribution, and in the year 399 B.C., five years after ruinous defeat in war and the rise of a murderous oligarchy, the Thirty Tyrants, Athens must have felt the hand of God already heavy upon her.

Still, impiety lay usually for a well-defined class of wrongs: for profanation of the Eleusinian Mysteries, for mutilation of sacred objects, for blasphemy or sacrilege affecting the religion of the City. Socrates was guilty of none of these. Impiety did not in general lie for unorthodoxy in belief; Athens was singularly free of the unlovely habit of persecuting men for their opinions, and indeed, it would be

17

difficult to say what religious orthodoxy at Athens consisted in. Athenian religion was not a matter of creed and dogma, but of ritual observance, of *dromena*, things done, rather than *legomena*, things said—appropriately enough, given a polytheistic theology whose doctrinal content, to the degree that it might be said to have any, consisted mainly in the myths of Homer and Hesiod. Impiety, in short, normally lay for definite kinds of acts.

The reach of the writ appears to have been extended by the prosecution of Anaxagoras, philosopher and friend of Pericles, perhaps some forty years earlier. Anaxagoras was tried, fined, and exiled from Athens for saying that the sun was stone and the moon was earth, and thus neither (by implication) the gods which tradition accepted them to be. But the trial—if indeed it took place—had been politically inspired as a way of striking at Pericles through his friends, and it appears to have required special legislation, the so-called psephism of Diopeithes,[1] to bring the case within the writ.

The case of Anaxagoras was remembered: Meletus actually confuses him with Socrates at one point (*Apology* 28d-e). But Socrates did not teach what Anaxagoras taught, and indeed, there is no evidence that he taught about religious matters at all, though there is clear evidence in the *Euthyphro* and elsewhere that he asked questions about theology embarrassing to Olympian fundamentalists. Still, Socrates had walked his peculiar way for many years without attracting a charge, and this could not have been so if his conduct fell within any clearly defined standard of wrong.

The claim that Socrates did not acknowledge the gods the City acknowledged seems to have rested on little more than his reputation as a sophist. Certainly he questioned the more gory and immoral tales told in Homer and Hesiod of the gods; but that, after all, was commonplace among educated Athenians in the late fifth century. The charge that he introduced new or strange divinities rested solely on his peculiar Sign. There is not enough in all this to explain how he came to attract an indictment for impiety, let alone a finding of guilt.

In short, the charges of irreligion against Socrates probably had a procedural rather than a substantive effect: they served to bring his conduct within the reach of a writ of impiety. The heart of the charge against him—and this is confirmed by the controversy over the verdict afterward—was corrupting the youth.

Hyperides, a younger contemporary of Plato born about 390 B.C., remarked that, "Our ancestors punished Socrates for what he said [*epi logois*]."[2] This was true, but the truth did not stand and work alone. Aeschines, fifty years after the trial, suggested that Athens put

Socrates to death because he had been teacher of Critias, one of the Thirty Tyrants;[3] Charmides, a member of the Socratic circle in his youth, was also among that unholy number.[4] Still another associate of Socrates was Alcibiades, brilliant and unrestrained, who turned traitor to his country during the Peloponnesian War. The sophist Polycrates cited his example in his "Accusation of Socrates," a set speech written in or after 393 B.C., since it mentioned the rebuilding of the long walls between Athens and the Piraeus under Conon. Isocrates roundly condemned the speech as bad rhetoric in the *Busiris*:

And when your purpose was to accuse Socrates, as if you wished to praise him, you gave Alcibiades to him as a pupil who, so far as anybody observed, never was taught by Socrates, but that Alcibiades far excelled all his contemporaries all would agree. Hence, if the dead should acquire the power of judging what has been said of them, Socrates would be as grateful to you for your accusation as to any who have been wont to eulogize him.[5]

But it is safe to say that in 399 B.C., most Athenians thought otherwise.[6]

We do not have Meletus's speech of accusation, nor the speeches of the supporting witnesses, Anytus and Lycon. The names of Critias, Charmides, and Alcibiades may not have been so much as directly mentioned. Indeed, the terms of the amnesty proclaimed when the democracy was restored after the overthrow of the Thirty would have forbidden it—though this did not in fact prevent such things from becoming commonplace in the law courts. Still, the charge of corrupting the youth would have been without effect (cf. *Apology* 33d-34a) had Meletus and those around him not been able to count on the appropriate examples springing nimbly—if not airily—to mind. Socrates' conduct under the Thirty was heroic (32c-e),[7] and widely known. The fact remained that he was tied to leading members of the Thirty, and to Alcibiades, a brilliant traitor, in remembered association.

Still, all this will not explain why, in 399, Socrates was brought to trial. The *Clouds* was an important source of prejudice; but the *Clouds* was first produced in 423. Alcibiades was Socrates' associate; but that was long before the disastrous Sicilian Expedition of 415. Critias and Charmides were also associates; but the Thirty fell in 404/3, and Socrates was not tried until 399. Four or five years, politically, is a long time, and more is required to account for the time lapse than busy courts and crowded dockets. Then too, there was the general amnesty issued after the Thirty fell. Charges might stick through past history. They were prompted by present offense.

Plato exhibits the nature of that offense in the *Meno*, in a discussion between Socrates and Anytus, soon to be one of the principle witnesses against him (*Meno* 89e-95a). The dramatic date of the dialogue is probably the early months of 402, and it is significant that Anytus, a leader of the restored democracy, was a political moderate.[8] But his hatred of Sophists runs deep, and Socrates comes very near to baiting him about it (cf. *Meno* 91b-d). Anytus' belief that the citizenry of Athens offers education in virtue—a traditional piece of democratic piety reaffirmed by Meletus in the *Apology* (24d-25a)—is subjected to calm and merciless criticism, which cuts the more deeply for its very lightness of touch: men held up as virtuous cannot teach their own sons virtue. How then can they teach others? In issuing this criticism, Socrates chooses as examples the democratic worthies of Athens' Golden Age—Themistocles, Pericles, and the rest—and Anytus, angered far out of proportion to anything which has been said, accuses Socrates of slander and issues a veiled threat. The threat is interesting: "Beware. It may be that in other cities too it is easier to do evil to men than good. Certainly it is in this one" (*Meno*, 94e). The very intensity of Anytus' emotion, and its disproportionateness in the circumstances, is itself significant. So it is that Socrates in the *Apology* (21c-22a) tells how he went to the politicians, and later the poets and craftsmen, and questioned them, and made them angry, and became hated.

Their anger, in its unreasonableness, came from something more than wounded pride. It was a time when the fabric of shared loyalties and beliefs which serve to bind a people had been rent; and if for nearly five years past that fabric had been patched, it was very far from mended. A quiet, gathered people can accept criticism of their ways with tolerance, and even a smile. But a people hammered apart on the anvil of events and then regathered has known fear, and Socrates' criticism roused memories of past danger:

But, said his accuser, he taught his companions to despise the established laws by insisting on the folly of appointing public officials by lot, when no one would choose a pilot or a builder or flautist by lot, nor any other craftsman for work on which mistakes are far less dangerous than mistakes in statecraft. Such sayings, he argued, lead the young to despise the established constitution and make them violent.[9]

Election by lot was a typical device of Athenian democracy; and if Socrates was less concerned with the luck of the draw than the folly and ignorance of popular assemblies and the deceitful, flattering rhetoric of their leaders, the point still holds. He touched, even in his very speech of defense, the most powerful and terrible of all political motives: fear, whose image is anger. He did not walk away alive.

The reasons for finding him guilty may be cast into a kind of syllogism. Impiety threatens the safety of the City; Socrates threatens the safety of the City; therefore, Socrates is impious. Popular emotion, the grudging slander of the Many represented in all its unreasoning intensity by Anytus, is not stayed in its course by logic. Socrates went to his death on the basis of an undistributed middle—or, if you will, a middle distributed only by anger and fear. The gadfly was swatted.

The Issue of Legality

The history books tell us that, "In equity Socrates was innocent. In Attic law he was guilty of the charge preferred against him."[1] Let us see.

Certainly Socrates was guilty if guilt is construed formally, and follows on being found guilty. A verdict in a court of law is not simply a true or false statement, but an operative fact, and in the absence of fresh evidence or invalid procedure, a verdict of guilt, however false to fact, implies guilt at law. No irregularity in the proceedings against Socrates was remarked either at the time or afterward. The evidence, such as it was, was in. By Athenian standards of due process, Socrates was convicted according to due process of law.

Still, it is possible to question the legal quality of the conviction. There are two principles which may reasonably be supposed to be implied in the very enterprise of law, at least insofar as it applies to the criminal process. There is a principle of procedural fairness: that no free man—*nullus liber homo*, to quote chapter 29 of *Magna Carta*—shall be subject to penal liability without notice and an opportunity to be heard before an impartial tribunal. There is a further principle, often called the principle of legality: that no free man shall be subject to penal liability imposed retroactively, nor except according to a clearly defined standard of wrong. These principles are broadly procedural; but they operate very much as though they were constitutional limitations.

The principle of legality and the principle of procedural fairness are directly and intimately connected. However it may be metaphysics, adjectives in law determine the effects of substance, as substance does of adjectives. The main vice excluded by the principle of legality is often taken to be retroactivity; in fact, I suggest, it is vagueness, for vagueness goes to proof. Notice of a vague charge, though it may allow you to prepare a defense which rests on persuasion—rhetoric—will not allow a defense which rests on proof, for there can be no proof where there is no clear standard error. A tribunal asked to adjudicate a vague charge can scarcely be said to be impartial: impartiality is not exhibited by disinterested coin-flipping. On the other hand, the principle of legality loses its sense apart from proof, and therefore apart from notice and hearing before an impartial tribunal. In short, where the principle of legality is not honored, procedural fairness is lost, even when it is on the surface provided for. The trial of Socrates provides a concrete example.

On the surface, at least, the requirements of procedural fairness were met. There was notice, hearing, and, to the degree that Athenian law could provide it, an impartial tribunal.

Notice was provided formally, by sworn information or indictment, and must have been preceded by personal service of summons. The indictment was laid under a recognized category of Athenian law, as a writ of impiety, and cited specific charges of irreligion and corrupting the youth. Adequate notice, it would seem, allowing Socrates an opportunity to prepare a defense.

The Athenian process required a preliminary hearing in cases of impiety before the King Archon, a magistrate charged with oversight of religious offenses, in whose discretion it lay whether to forward a case to trial. His function was analogous to that of a modern judge holding a preliminary inquiry to determine whether sufficient evidence —in the Athenian process, evidence both as to fact and law—existed to warrant further proceedings. We know from Plato's *Euthyphro* that Socrates appeared before the King in preliminary hearing, and was given opportunity to answer the charges against him. The King, in forwarding the case, had made a preliminary determination that the charges against Socrates, if true, tended to subvert worship in the city of Athena and, by endangering sacred custom, endangered the City itself. Presumably, he had also found sufficient evidence to indicate that trial should be made of the truth of the charges.

The trial itself was public—very public, since it took place before five hundred dicasts and a large and fractious audience. The dicasts were citizens functioning both as jurymen and judges, finding both fact and law—which law might be placed in evidence before them. Precautions were taken to ensure the impartiality of the tribunal. The dicasts were sworn to render judgment according to their true opinion, and the oath still retained, as at early common law, the force of a religious obligation (see *Apology* 35c). The dicasts were chosen by lot, and assigned to their respective courts immediately before trial in order to prevent tampering. The very size of their number, the fact that they were quite literally a popular court, itself had historical antecedents grounded in the quest for impartiality. Cases at one time had been tried by the magistrates alone. Solon, the great Athenian lawgiver of the sixth century, had introduced *ephesis*, a process of appeal or perhaps of removal and trial *de novo*, from the decision of magistrates to a popular court, the Heliaia, because of suspicion of oligarchical bias; and with the rapid development of democratic institutions in Athens in the fifth century, along with increased judicial business, that court was transformed into a plurality of courts of first instance. This history, in part at least, helps to explain what is otherwise difficult to understand, namely, that there was no appeal from the decision of an Athenian court in a criminal case in 399 B.C. When you had had your trial you had had your appeal, after the preliminary finding of the magistrate.

This was the more unfortunate because lack of provision for appeal led not only to unseemly but unfair haste in criminal cases; one function of appeal would have been to provide opportunity, not only for correction of error, but for sober second thought. The element of haste in the Athenian process was one which Socrates specifically condemned.[2]

If Athenian procedure did not conduce to second thoughts, the size of the jury scarcely conduced to thought at all. Gorgias defines rhetoric, at one point, as power of persuasion "in courts and other mobs" (*Gorgias* 453b, cf. 455a, *Euthydemus* 290a), and the technique of the popular orator involved much of applied mob psychology. Throughout the *Apology*, Socrates punctuates his speech with requests to his judges not to make a disturbance, and the number of his requests, if they indicate the frequency with which he says things he knows his audience will find outrageous, surely also indicates the turbulence with which he had to deal. Benjamin Bickley Rogers, barrister-at-law and translator of Aristophanes, remarked in his introduction to the *Wasps*:

I do not propose to discuss the general merits or demerits of the dicastic system. It may or may not have been found to operate advantageously for the political education of Athenian citizens, or otherwise for the benefit of the State; but I must record my opinion, as an English lawyer, that it would be difficult to devise a judicial system less adapted for the due administration of justice. A large Assembly can rarely, if ever, form a fit tribunal for ascertaining questions of fact, or deciding questions of law. Its members lose, to a great extent, their sense of individual responsibility, and it is apt to degenerate into a mere mob, open to all the influences, and liable to be swayed by all the passions, which stir and agitate popular meetings. . . . The members of the Heliastic assemblies had received no previous training whatever. They were not even selected with reference to their intellectual capacity or aptitude for the task. Taken at haphazard from the general community, and necessarily, as a rule, from the needy and less educated classes, they were at once elevated into supreme irresponsible judges, empowered in the name and with the authority of the Athenian People to decide finally and without appeal every question, whether of law or of fact, which might be brought before them. . . . What wonder then if the members of an Heliastic assembly were so constantly carried away by their feelings, that such a term as *thorubein, tumultari*, became almost a technical expression to denote their stormy uproarious agitations?[3]

We think of judicial proceedings as properly distinguished by ordered calm. The *Apology*, that reasoned speech of that most eminently reasonable of men, was delivered in an atmosphere very like a circus.

The trial itself was an adversary proceeding. Greek vocabulary on this point is interesting: the accuser was 'the pursuer' and the accused 'the fleer', metaphors which closely match our 'prosecutor' and 'defendant'; the trial itself was an *agon tes dikes*, a contest of right.[4] Socrates and his accusers were given equal time, measured by a water clock, to make their statements to the court. The rules of evidence were laxly enforced, as one might expect in a court of five hundred untrained judges, but rules there were. The accuser could be cross-examined on his charges, and was required by law to answer, as Socrates' examination of Meletus shows.[5] Witnesses could be summoned on both sides, and so, in a sense, might the dicasts, who could be requested to testify to each other;[6] this involved something more than judicial notice, for it went to contestable facts. Law could be entered in evidence, with threat of the death penalty for those who cited nonexistent law. Requirements of relevance were loose, and seem to have been served in criminal cases mainly by the water clock: you could say pretty much what you pleased, but you had a strictly limited time in which to say it. Thus it was that the *argumentum ad misericordiam* became so regular a feature of Athenian criminal trials, to Socrates' scornful condemnation.[7] Irrelevance apart, hearsay was in theory excluded, though it played its part in convicting Socrates,[8] and perjury was punished, though apparently only by civil action. There was no burden of proof, or more accurately, persuasion, nor was there any institutionalized analogue of it: conviction was obtained by the vote of a simple majority, with acquittal in case of a tie. The defense, however, spoke last, a very great advantage, and the prosecutor was fined if he failed to obtain a fifth part of the vote, a step taken to inhibit malicious prosecution. At this date at least, parties to a criminal action appear to have been required to plead personally, not by attorney (see *Apology* 19a), and rhetoric became a skill which many of the more well-to-do citizens found it advisable to acquire;[9] but there were *rhetors*, experts both in law and oratory, whom you could hire to brief your case and, indeed, write your speech for you. There is a tradition that Lysias, one of the best of them, offered to brief Socrates, and that Socrates refused.

So Socrates had notice and an opportunity to be heard before a tribunal meant to be impartial, though perhaps better described as impartial in its probable partiality. In a descriptive sense of due process, he was found guilty according to due process of law. But there is a special feature in the brief portrait of the Athenian trial process I have just drawn which is worth remarking. It is that law was pleaded in evidence:

We may find it strange that laws and decrees should be classed as evidence; we regard evidence as directed towards establishing the facts, while laws and decrees constitute the framework of rules under which the facts have to be subsumed. But in the Athenian courts of the fourth century there was no sharp distinction between decisions on law and on facts. Both were ultimately in the hands of the dicasts, and there was no judge experienced in the law whose task it was, with the help of advocates likewise experienced, to explicate the rules (of which laws would be the leading constituent) which should govern the decision on the facts. It was inevitable therefore that the litigant should have the duty of laying before the court any law or decree relevant to his case, whether he was plaintiff or defendant, and that the laws thus cited should come to be regarded as on all fours with evidence in convincing the dicasts to vote in his favour.[10]

Bentham condemned the arcane technicalities of "Judge & Co.," and urged that law should be "cognoscible." But there is an important distinction between mere legal underbrush and a benign technicality aimed at precision. Athenian law, at the trial stage at least, was magnificently untechnical, and eminently cognoscible to the lay intelligence. The result was to substitute rhetoric and persuasion for proof, and to open the door wide to the evils of vagueness.

Observe, please, the effect of this on a finding of legal guilt. A verdict, it will be said, contains a factual component. It is either true to fact or false. But what is meant by a 'fact'?

Take Jones and his burglary. Blackstone defines burglary as a breaking and entering of any dwelling-house by night with intent to commit felony, and he also defines those elements; the precision of his account is further protected by the principle that criminal law is to be construed strictly, so that what is not clearly within the definition is outside it. When Jones is charged with burglary and brought into court, the trier of fact is faced with a direct empirical question, to be settled on the basis of evidence, namely, Did he do it? A verdict of guilty is the answer, Yes, he did.

But then, the question "Did he do it?" presupposes that we know with some precision what 'it' is. A verdict involves not only a statement of fact, but a legal classification of fact, that is, a classification according to rules of law. If we are to impute burglary to Jones, we must find that he did given acts, and that those acts are of a kind subsumed under the rule forbidding burglary. Entering a dwelling-house by night is relevant; needing a shave and a haircut is not. A legal system which does not provide clear definition of the elements which go to constitute offenses will be characterized, in practice, by implicit and unannounced retroactivity; it will allow new elements to be imported into an offense—into a writ, given a formulary system of the sort which obtained in Athens—which do not provide an acknowledged and prospective basis for the charge. This sort of retroactivity does not arise from the retrospective application of a clearly defined rule; there, the violation of the principle of legality is obvious. It arises from the apparently and deceptively prospective application of an unclearly defined rule, a rule whose elements are unsettled at the circumference. This is basically a kind of vagueness; and because it will serve not only to convict those who have had no prospective warning of a charge, but also to deter those who find themselves without basis for predicting when they may attract a charge, it involves a type of over-breadth which is in two ways destructive of liberty. Given a developed principle of *stare decisis*, this sort of vagueness can be cured, piece by piece and bit by bit, after the fact; retrospective delineation of the contours of an offense will in the long run yield considerable clarity of definition. Nor need this retrospectivity sin against legality, so long as it consists in expanding a rule to the reach of its proximate reason, for it is the reason, not the technical expression of the rule, which is in general understood by those to whom the law is directed. But an Athenian court was unbound, except persuasively, by precedent: the elements of impiety were what a simple majority of dicasts on any given day thought was impious. There was no cure, not even after the fact, and the reasons entertained by the court might be as broad as 'general social welfare'—or mere prejudice.[11]

Unsettled elements in an offense may at least allow proof according to empirical standards of fact. It is otherwise when the elements themselves are undefined, when they are vague as lacking any clear standard of application. The trier of fact is then at large in determining what kind of fact he is to try, and the very notion that verdicts rest on fact will require some modification. A trial is a search for truth. But what kind of truth? When the search is no longer to determine whether given acts satisfy determinate conditions for the application of a rule, the inquiry will enlarge into questions about what may loosely be called 'conduct' rather than action, about the character of the man you are dealing with, and whether you approve or disapprove. That is, questions of innocence and guilt will come to be settled, not on the basis of what he did or didn't do, but on the basis of the kind of man you think he is.

Facts, in short, are a function of the legal rules by which they are classified, and if those rules are vague and ill-defined, the facticity of facts—if I may so speak—will be commensurately affected. And since proof is a function of fact, degeneration of fact-requirements will lead to degeneration of proof-requirements. Trials we may still have, but their outcome will turn on rhetoric and persuasion—specifically persuasion about what a fine fellow you are and what a nasty fellow your opponent is—rather than empirically ascertainable standards of proof. This description matches the actual course of Greek pleading, and was reinforced by a further distinction which became a pleader's trick. Law, *nomos*, that which is dealt or distributed or alloted, is ambiguous between written law and custom, or unwritten law; and some part of the latter came to be idealized as equity, universal principles of justice common to all men, in the same way the Romans later associated *ius naturale* with *ius gentium*. Here is how the distinction worked in practice in a Greek court:

If the written law tells against our case, clearly we must appeal to the universal law, and insist on its greater equity and justice. We must argue that the juror's oath 'I will give my verdict according to my honest opinion' means that one will not simply follow the letter of the written law. . . . If however the written law supports our case, we must argue that the oath . . . is not meant to make judges give a verdict which is contrary to law.[12]

The court is at large, not only as to what it will consider fact, or how it will interpret law, but even as to what it will consider law. Aristotle, in the foregoing quotation, is explaining how to use laws as the instruments of persuasion.

The result was a truly terrible gap between rhetoric and reality, between what Athens believed of herself and what she in fact was. Here is Pericles on democracy in the *Funeral Oration*:

> It is true that we are called a democracy, for the administration is in the hands of the many and not of the few. But while the law secures equal justice to all alike in their private disputes, the claim of excellence is also recognized; and when a citizen is in any way distinguished, he is preferred to the public service, not as a matter of privilege, but as the reward of merit. Neither is poverty a bar, but a man may benefit his country whatever be the obscurity of his condition. There is no exclusiveness in our public life, and in our private intercourse we are not suspicious of one another, nor angry with our neighbor if he does what he likes; we do not put on sour looks at him which, though harmless, are not pleasant. While we are thus unconstrained in our private intercourse, a spirit of reverence pervades our public acts; we are prevented from doing wrong by respect for the authorities and for the laws, having an especial regard to those which are ordained for the protection of the injured as well as to those unwritten laws which bring upon the transgressors of them the reprobation of the general sentiment.[13]

Plato, who knew his Thucydides and had seen the trial of Socrates, satirized this passage in the *Menexenus* (238c-239a), in the course of a funeral oration which he feigned to have been delivered by Pericles' hetaera, Aspasia.

Return then to the claim that though in equity Socrates was innocent, he was guilty in Athenian law. Guilty by what standards of guilt? The answer is, guilty by no standards at all, except the formal one of having been voted guilty. Socrates died, not because of what he did, but because he was the kind of man he was. His trial was, in effect, a political trial, and the fact that it could take place as it did constitutes a severe indictment of the legal quality of Athenian law. Samuel Eliot Morison, the distinguished student of American history, once remarked that a legal system must in the long run be judged by the extremes it will tolerate. We deal here with an extreme.

Where the principle of legality is seriously infringed, procedural fairness is lost. If Plato's account of Socrates' speech of defense is accurate, it illustrates the point. Socrates did not deny the charges against him. He did not because he could not: and there was a legal reason why he could not. Quite apart from the philosophical or dialectical issue of what piety and impiety are, the charges against him provided no legal standard by which ascertainable fact could be adduced to support or refute them: they admitted neither proof nor disproof. This is a further, and central, reason for "the Silence of Socrates." He is not silent where questions of fact are concerned: for example, that he never taught for pay. But he is compelled to conduct his defense, not on the issue of whether he had broken a legal rule to which facts are intrinsically relevant, but on the issue of whether or not he was socially undesirable. That is why his speech mainly deals, not with the formal charges brought against him and under which he is nominally tried, but with prejudice arising from informal accusations going back more than twenty years, popularly circulated, and based on ripest hearsay. He is primarily defending himself, not against an indictment, but against prejudice founded on slander, and against the widely held view that he was a threat to the established order of things. This, in practice, is what notice and an opportunity to be heard before an impartial tribunal had boiled down to.

To sum up. In a legal system in which rules of criminal law are so loosely defined that it is difficult to say in given cases what specific acts, if any, constitute a breach of them, innocence and guilt lose precise meaning, as does proof. Impiety in Athens had a relatively clear center—mutilation of sacred objects, for example—but a vague circumference, so that in given cases it could only be defined at law as what a bare majority of dicasts thought to be impious. The Athenian legal system had no check on whether they did right to think so; its procedure did not, and could not, cure defective substance. Instead, it aggravated it. So it was that persuasion was substituted for proof, and condemnation for guilt. And so it was that Socrates died a condemned criminal. A procedure requiring laymen to find not only fact but law is incompatible with the technical precision required by legality.

Socrates was tried under an adversary system. But there is no single process properly called *the* adversary system, and the Athenian version allowed justice to be administered by an organized mob. Ideally, an adversary system involves more than people fighting each other in a courtroom or even fighting each other according to rule. It involves the strenuous assertion of rights claimed under principles of legal rationality, of which legality and procedural fairness are essential parts, as a bulwark against the exercise of arbitrary power, whether of the many or the few. As Aristotle put it long ago, "To invest the law with authority is, it seems, to invest God and reason only; to invest a man is to introduce a beast, as desire is something bestial, and even the best of men in authority are liable to be corrupted by passion. We may conclude that law is reason without passion and is preferable to any individual."[14] To a degree that Aristotle did not and could not realize, the reason he extolled was what Coke once called, in a memorable interview with James I, "the artificial reason and judgement of the law,"[15] 'artificial', not as feigned or fictitious, but as proceeding according to rules of art, rules aimed at proof, at fact, at legality, at procedural fairness. It is that artifact which gives content to the ancient ideal of a government of laws, not men, and to the inestimable good of liberty under law.

The trial of Socrates stands as both symbol and symptom of failure in the Athenian polity. James Madison, a close student of ancient constitutions, gave a concise and accurate diagnosis of the difficulty in Number 10 of the *Federalist*, that much neglected masterpiece of applied political theory:

[A] pure democracy, by which I mean a society consisting in a small number of citizens, who assemble and administer the government in person, can admit of no cure for the mischiefs of faction. A common passion or interest will, in almost every case, be felt by a majority of the whole; a communication and concert result from the form of government itself; and there is nothing to check the inducements to sacrifice the weaker party or an obnoxious individual. Hence it is that such democracies have ever been spectacles of turbulence and contention; have ever been found incompatible with personal security or the rights of property; and have in general been as short in their lives as they have been violent in their deaths.

The analysis resembles that of *Republic* VIII. Madison neglects to add, as Plato did, that democracy, reduced to anarchy, becomes tyranny—perhaps because the rule of a majority unchecked by law, Madison thought, is already a form of tryanny in itself.

Dean Pound described Athenian law as a species of primitive law which was yet peculiarly conducive to the study of jurisprudence: "the uncertainty with respect to form and the want of uniformity in application, which are characteristic of primitive law, . . . invited thought as to the reality behind such confusion."[16] Whether Athenian law was in fact primitive, as aboriginal and undeveloped, or whether it merely seems primitive because it became in the fifth century so heavily politicized, is a question worth exploring. But certainly the trial of Socrates had the beneficent effect of stimulating further reflection on jurisprudence, which Sophocles in the *Antigone* had begun and which, if the *Crito* may be taken as historically faithful, Socrates was still to carry forward.

A concluding remark. Athenian law was surely law. But if law is, as Professor Lon Fuller suggests, an enterprise of subjecting human conduct to the governance of rules,[17] it is also possible to say that Athenian law, because of its procedural inadequacies, fell short of lawfulness, that in operation it was too often a specimen of lawless law. There are those who claim to find in the notion of 'lawless law' a contradition in terms. But it describes a fact of everyday occurrence. Law is not morals. Indeed, one of the things wrong with Athenian law was too large an injection of the of the loose and emotive standards of popular morality. But it is worth asking, with Fuller, whether there is not an inner morality of law itself, as an enterprise whose purpose is to govern conduct by rules, and whether legality and procedural fairness are not essential elements of that morality. No doubt, as Professor H. L. A. Hart has argued,[18] those elements are unfortunately compatible with very great iniquity. Yet with them, even a slave under a slave code is guaranteed important rights. It is surely reasonable to hold that where those rights are denied, there is denial of law, and that law which countenances such denial is, by so much, law which falls short of its own inner aim, and thus falls short of what it is to be law.

The Issue of Historicity

Plato's *Apology* purports to represent a historical occurrence, namely, the speech which Socrates made at his trial. It is a natural question, and one often asked, whether Plato's representation of that speech is accurate to historical fact.

There is a kind of conventional wisdom which has grown up as an answer. Shorey expressed it as well as anyone:

> The discussion of the 'historicity' of Socrates' speech to his judges naively assumes that the *Dichtung und Wahrheit* of Plato's art was controlled by the critical conscience of a modern historian. Socrates may or may not have said some of the things attributed to him by Plato who was present. Plato could easily imitate, so far as he pleased, the forms and phrases of Athenian courtroom oratory. But there is no likelihood that just such a speech as the *Apology* was ever delivered to an Athenian jury. It is too obviously Plato's idealization of his master's life and mission and his summing-up of the things that needed to be said to the Athenian public about his condemnation by a democratic tribunal.[1]

With respect, I propose to argue that within such limits of proof as the subject matter admits, this answer is provably mistaken, and that as a matter of best evidence, we should accept the *Apology* as essentially accurate. No doubt best evidence and truth are different things, and the gods on Olympus may sometimes laugh, or weep, to hear historians argue. But this is merely to say that arguments from best evidence are inductive, and yield probability rather than certainty.

To begin with, a *caveat*. By saying that the *Apology* is essentially accurate, I do not mean that it is a word-for-word presentation of Socrates' speech. There is textual reason to doubt that. At *Crito* 45b, Crito says that Socrates said at his trial that if he left, "he would not know what to do with himself." The expression is idiomatic; it has the ring of quotation; it fits the sense of *Apology* 37c-e; but it is not found there. Again, at *Crito* 52c, the Laws of Athens say that Socrates said at his trial that he preferred death to exile. This may be implied by *Apology* 37c-e, but is nowhere explicitly stated. So there is good reason to suppose that the *Apology* is not a stenographic report, even though Plato takes pains to indicate that he was present and heard the speech (34a, 38b), a thing he does nowhere else in the dialogues. To say that the *Apology* is essentially accurate is not to say that it is word-for-word, but that it reproduces the general substance of what Socrates said, and the way he said it.

Let us take a negative point first. There is no good evidence that the *Apology* is inaccurate to the speech. I shall simply assume on the basis of what has gone before that this is true internally of the *Apology* itself and its coherence with other early dialogues, and deal with external evidence.

We may begin by setting aside the "Accusation of Socrates" written by the Sophist Polycrates sometime after 393 B.C., and criticized by Isocrates in the *Busiris* (paras. 5–6). Our knowledge of this speech is only fragmentary; but it was a sophistical *epideixis*, a set-speech, and explicitly referred to Socrates' association with Alcibiades as a matter of reproach. This sort of reference should have been excluded in court, according to the terms of the amnesty issued by the restored democracy after the fall of the Thirty. If it does not thereby follow that it was in fact excluded, neither does it follow, as a matter of evidence, that the speech of Polycrates had any close relation to the original speeches of Socrates' accusers, and still less to the original speech of Socrates himself.

Next, we may set aside the Hellenistic tradition that Socrates at his trial stood mute. This, as we have seen, is a mistaken interpretation of Plato's *Gorgias*. It is contradicted by all of the direct contemporary evidence that we have, namely, Plato's *Apology*, Xenophon's *Apology*, and Isocrates' *Antidosis*.

We come now to Xenophon's *Apology*. This both conflicts with Plato's *Apology* and in a crucial respect confirms it. The fact which Xenophon sets out to explain is the fact of *megalegoria*, loftiness of speech or big talk. That fact is amply attested in Plato's *Apology*.

Xenophon, of course, is not an independent witness. He was not present at the trial, and he confesses in his first paragraph that he does not know what was said except insofar as it was written about. He can explain the *megalegoria*, which he finds universally attested, only in intellectual impoverished terms: it is aimed at suicide by judicial process.[2] If this is a mere perversion of Plato's account, it is also indirect testimony to the accuracy of the most single striking feature of that account, namely, a tone which verges on arrogance. Thus, Xenophon's account, however far it may diverge from Plato in its explanation, confirms Plato's account in respect to the fact to be explained.

The strongest external evidence of the accuracy of Plato's account is Isocrates' *Antidosis*.

Isocrates knew Socrates[3] and admired him, as the *Antidosis* itself shows. There is an ancient tradition that he was deeply grieved at his death and put on mourning for him;[4] in the circumstances, this would have been no light thing to do. There is no reason to suppose that Isocrates was not thoroughly familiar with the events of the trial; he was at the time a grown man, having been born in 436 B.C. The *Antidosis* was written in or around 354 B.C., and it is surely no accident that Isocrates, in constructing his own *apologia pro sua vita*, imitates Plato's *Apology*. The late Professor Norlin writes,

(Isocrates) adopts the fiction of a capital charge brought against him by an informer, named Lysimachus, and of a trial before a court with its accessories. The fictitious charge is, roughly, that he is guilty of corrupting his pupils by teaching them to make the worse reason appear the better and so to win their advantage contrary to justice, which is the stock complaint against the sophists, and the one which was pressed against Socrates. Indeed, it is clear that Isocrates had the latter's trial in mind and that he studiously echoes the defence of Socrates as it is recorded by Plato in the *Apology*.[5]

That the *Antidosis* echoes the *Apology*, and constantly so, is indisputable.[6] But Isocrates means to compare himself, surely, to Socrates, not to Plato's portrait of Socrates. It follows that Isocrates, who was in a position to know, must have supposed that Plato's *Apology* is essentially accurate to the speech which Socrates gave.

To sum up. There is no good evidence that the *Apology* is inaccurate. There is good evidence that the *Apology* is accurate. Therefore, as a matter of best evidence, we must accept the *Apology* as accurate.

This need hardly occasion surprise. Plato could have had no good reason for presenting an account of Socrates' defense at variance with the facts to an audience thoroughly familiar with what Socrates had actually said. If you believe that Socrates, as well as Plato, was a man of genius; if you believe that Socrates could easily parody the sophists and outdo them in eloquence, as in the stunning speech interpreting Simonides he is made to offer in the *Protagoras* (342a-347a); if you believe that Socrates cared deeply to know what piety and virtue are, and knew that he did not know; if you believe that his ignorance, combined with the state of the law, prevented him from denying the charges brought against him—if you believe all these things, then it is open to you to believe not only that Socrates could have made essentially the speech which Plato presents, but perhaps also that he could have made no other. The distinction between rhetoric aimed at flattery and rhetoric aimed at truth must have been very early forced on his mind; if the result represents 'idealization', it is perhaps because the ideal was there.

The Apology

INTRODUCTION

17a To what degree, Gentlemen of Athens, you have been affected by my accusers, I do not know. I, at any rate, was almost led to forget who I am—so convincingly did they speak. Yet hardly anything they have said is true. Among their many falsehoods, I was especially surprised by one; they said you must be on guard lest I deceive you, since I am a clever speaker. To

b have no shame at being directly refuted by facts when I show myself in no way clever with words—that, I think, is the very height of shamelessness. Unless, of course, they call a man a clever speaker if he speaks the truth. If that is what they mean, why, I would even admit to being an orator—though not after *their* fashion.

These men, I claim, have said little or nothing true. But from me, Gentlemen, you will hear the whole truth. It will not be prettily tricked out in elegant speeches like theirs,

c words and phrases all nicely arranged. To the contrary: you will hear me speak naturally in the words which happen to occur to me. For I believe what I say to be just, and let no one of you expect otherwise. Besides, it would hardly be appropriate in a man of my age, Gentlemen, to come before you making up speeches like a boy.[1] So I must specifically ask one thing of you, Gentlemen. If you hear me make my defense in the same words I customarily use at the tables in the Agora, and other places where many of you have heard me, please do

d not be surprised or make a disturbance because of it. For things stand thus: I am now come into court for the first time; I am seventy years old; and I am an utter stranger to this place. If I were a foreigner, you would unquestionably make

18a allowances if I spoke in the dialect and manner in which I was raised. In just the same way, I specifically ask you now, and justly so, I think, to pay no attention to my manner of speech —it may perhaps be poor, but then perhaps an improvement— and look strictly to this one thing, whether or not I speak justly. For that is the virtue of a judge, and the virtue of an orator is to speak the truth.

STATEMENT

First of all, Gentlemen, it is right for me to defend myself against the first false accusations lodged against me, and my first accusers; and next, against later accusations and later ac-

b cusers. For the fact is that many accusers have risen before you against me; at this point they have been making accusations for many years, and they have told no truth. Yet I fear them more than I fear Anytus and those around him—though they too are dangerous. Still, the others are more dangerous. They took hold of most of you in childhood, persuading you of the truth of accusations which were in fact quite false: "There is a certain Socrates . . . Wise man . . . Thinker on things in the Heavens . . . Inquirer into all things beneath Earth . . . Making the weaker argument stronger. . . . " Those

c men, Gentlemen of Athens, the men who spread that report, are my dangerous accusers; for their hearers believe that those who inquire into such things acknowledge no gods.

Again, there have been many such accusers, and they have now been at work for a long time; they spoke to you at a time when you were especially trusting—some of you children, some only a little older—and they lodged their accusations quite by default, no one appearing in defense. But the most absurd

d thing is that one cannot even know or tell their names—unless perhaps in the case of a comic poet.[2] But those who use malicious slander to persuade you, and those who, themselves persuaded, persuade others—all are most difficult to deal with. For it is impossible to bring any one of them forward as a witness and cross-examine him. I must rather, as it were, fight with shadows in making my defense, and question where no one answers.

Please grant, then, as I say, that two sets of accusers have risen against me: those who now lodge their accusations, and those who lodged accusations long since. And please accept the fact that I must defend myself against the latter first. For in fact, you heard their accusations earlier, and with far greater effect than those which came later.

Very well then. A defense is to be made, Gentlemen of Athens. I am to attempt to remove from you this short time that prejudice which you have been long in acquiring. I might wish that this should come to pass, if it were in some way better for you and for me, wish that I might succeed in my defense. But I think the thing difficult, and its nature hardly escapes me. Still, let that go as pleases the God; the law must be obeyed, and a defense conducted.

REFUTATION OF THE OLD ACCUSERS

Let us then take up from the beginning the charges which have given rise to the prejudice—the charges on which Meletus in fact relied in lodging his indictment. Very well, what do those who slander me say? It is necessary to read, as it were, their sworn indictment: "Socrates is guilty of needless curiosity and meddling interference, inquiring into things beneath Earth and in the Sky, making the weaker argument stronger, and teaching others the same." The charge is something like that. Indeed, you have seen it for yourselves in a comedy by Aristophanes— a certain Socrates being carried around on the stage, talking about walking on air and babbling a great deal of other nonsense, of which I understand neither much nor little. Mark you, I do not mean to disparage such knowledge, if anyone in fact has it—let me not be brought to trial by Meletus on such a charge as that! But Gentlemen, I have no share of it. Once again, I offer the majority of you as witnesses, and ask those of you who have heard me in conversation—there are many among you—inform each other, please, whether any of you ever heard anything of the sort. From that you will recognize the nature of the other things the multitude says about me.

The fact is that there is nothing in these accusations. And if you have heard from anyone that I undertake to educate men, and make money doing it, that is false too. Once again, I think it would be a fine thing to be able to educate men, as Gorgias of Leontini does, or Prodicus of Ceos, or Hippias of Elis. For each of them, Gentlemen, can enter any given city and convince the youth—who might freely associate with any of their fellow citizens they please—to drop those associations and associate with them, to pay money for it, and give thanks in the bargain. As a matter of fact, there is a man here right now, a Parian, and a wise one, who as I learn has just come to town. For I happened to meet a person who has spent more money on Sophists than everyone else put together, Callias, son of Hipponicus. So I asked him—for he has two sons— "Callias, " I said, "if your two sons were colts or calves, we could get an overseer for them and hire him, and his business would be to make them excellent in their appropriate virture. He would be either a horse-trainer or a farmer. But as it is, since the two of them are men, whom do you intend to get as an overseer? Who has knowledge of that virtue which belongs to a man and a citizen? Since you have sons, I'm sure you have considered this. Is there such a person," I said, "or not?"

"To be sure," he said.

"Who is he?" I said. "Where is he from, and how much does he charge to teach?"

"Evenus, Socrates," he said. "A Parian. Five minae."[3]

And I count Evenus fortunate indeed, if he really possesses that art, and teaches it so modestly. For my own part, at any rate, I would be puffed up with vanity and pride if I had such knowledge. But I do not, Gentlemen.

Perhaps one of you will ask, "But Socrates, what is this all about? Whence have these slanders against you arisen? You must surely have been busying yourself with something out of the ordinary; so grave a report and rumor would not have arisen had you not been doing something rather different from most folk. Tell us what it is, so that we may not take action in your case unadvisedly." That, I think, is a fair request, and I shall try to indicate what it is that has given me the name I have. Hear me, then. Perhaps some of you will think I joke; be well assured that I shall be telling the whole truth.

Gentlemen of Athens, I got this name through nothing but a kind of wisdom. What kind? The kind which is perhaps peculiarly human, for it may be I am really wise in that. And perhaps the men I just mentioned are wise with a wisdom greater than human—either that, or I cannot say what. In any case, I have no knowledge of it, and whoever says I do is lying and speaks to my slander.

e

Please, Gentlemen of Athens. Do not make a disturbance, even if I seem to you to boast. For it will not be my own words I utter; I shall refer you to the speaker, as one worthy of credit. For as witness to you of my wisdom—whether it is wisdom of a kind, and what kind of wisdom it is—I shall call the God at Delphi.

You surely knew Chaerephon. He was my friend from youth, and a friend of your democratic majority. He went into exile with you,[4] and with you he returned. And you know what kind of a man he was, how eager and impetuous in whatever he rushed into. Well, he once went to Delphi and boldly asked the oracle—as I say, Gentlemen, please do not make a disturbance—he asked whether anyone is wiser than I. Now, the Pythia[5] replied that no one is wiser. And to this his brother here will testify, since Chaerephon is dead.

21a

b

Why do I mention this? I mention it because I intend to inform you whence the slander against me has arisen. For when I heard it, I reflected: "What does the God mean? What is the sense of this riddling utterance? I know that I am not wise at all; what then does the God mean by saying I am wisest? Surely he does not speak falsehood; it is not permitted to him." So I puzzled for a long time over what was meant, and then, with great reluctance, I turned to inquire into the matter in some such way as this.

c

I went to someone with a reputation for wisdom, in the belief that there if anywhere I might test the meaning of the utterance and declare to the oracle that, "This man is wiser than I am, and you said I was wisest." So I examined him—there is no need to mention a name, but it was someone in political life who produced this effect on me in discussion, Gentlemen of Athens—and I concluded that though he seemed wise to many other men, and most especially to himself, he was not. I tried to show him this; and thence I became hated, by him and by many who were present. But I left thinking to myself, "I am wiser than that man. Neither of us probably

d

knows anything worthwhile; but he thinks he does and does
not, and I do not and do not think I do. So it seems at any
rate that I am wiser in this one small respect: I do not think I
know what I do not." I then went to another man who was
reputed to be even wiser, and the same thing seemed true

e   again; there too I became hated, by him and by many others.

Nevertheless, I went on, perceiving with grief and fear that
I was becoming hated, but still, it seemed necessary to put the
God first—so I had to go on, examining what the oracle meant

22a   by testing everyone with a reputation for knowledge. And by
the Dog,[6] Gentlemen—I must tell you the truth—I swear that
I had some such experience as this: it seemed to me that those
most highly esteemed for wisdom fell little short of being
most deficient, as I carried on inquiry in behalf of the God,
and that others reputedly inferior were men of more discern-
ment.

But really, I must display my wanderings to you; they were
like those of a man performing labors[7]—all to the end that I
might not leave the oracle untested. From the politicians I
went to the poets—tragic, dithyrambic, and the rest—thinking

b   that there I would discover myself manifestly less wise by
comparison. So I took up poems over which I thought they
had taken special pains, and asked them what they meant, so
as also at the same time to learn from them. Now, I am
ashamed to tell you the truth, Gentlemen, but still, it must
be told. There was hardly anyone present who could not give
a better account than they of what they had themselves pro-

c   duced. So presently I came to realize that poets do not make
what they make by wisdom, but by a kind of native disposi-
tion or divine inspiration, exactly like seers and prophets. For
the latter also utter many fine things, but know nothing of
the things of which they speak. That is how the poets also appeared to me, while at the same time I realized that because
of their poetry they thought themselves the wisest of men in
other matters—and were not. Once again, I left thinking myself superior to them in just the way I was to the politicians.

Finally I went to the craftsmen. I was aware that although
I knew scarcely anything, I would find that they knew many
things, and fine ones. In this I was not mistaken: they knew
things that I did not, and in that respect were wiser. But Gentlemen of Athens, it seemed to me that the poets and our capa-

ble public craftsmen had exactly the same failing: because they practiced their own arts well, each deemed himself wise in other things, things of great importance. This mistake quite obscured their wisdom. The result was that I asked myself on behalf of the oracle whether I would accept being such as I am, neither wise with their wisdom nor foolish with their folly, or whether I would accept wisdom and folly together and become such as they are. I answered, both for myself and the oracle, that it was better to be as I am.

From this examination, Gentlemen of Athens, much enmity has risen against me, of a sort most harsh and heavy to endure, so that many slanders have arisen, and the name is put abroad that I am 'wise'. For on each occasion those present think I am wise in the things in which I test others. But very likely, Gentlemen, it is really the God who is wise, and by his oracle he means to say that, "Human nature is a thing of little worth, or none." It appears that he does not mean this fellow Socrates, but uses my name to offer an example, as if he were saying that, "He among you, Gentlemen, is wisest who, like Socrates, realizes that he is truly worth nothing in respect to wisdom." That is why I still go about even now on behalf of the God, searching and inquiring among both citizens and strangers, should I think some one of them is wise; and when it seems he is not, I help the God and prove it. Due to this pursuit, I have no leisure worth mentioning either for the affairs of the City or for my own estate; I dwell in utter poverty because of my service to God.

Then too the young men follow after me—especially the ones with leisure, namely, the richest. They follow of their own initiative, rejoicing to hear men tested, and often they imitate me and undertake to test others; and next, I think, they find an ungrudging plenty of people who think they have some knowledge but know little or nothing. As a result, those whom they test become angry at me, not at themselves, and say that, "This fellow Socrates is utterly polluted, and corrupts the youth." And when someone asks them what it is he does, what it is he teaches, they cannot say because they do not know; but so as not to seem at a loss, they mutter the kind of thing that lies ready to hand against anyone who pursues wisdom: "Things in the Heavens and beneath the Earth," or, "Not acknowledging gods," or, "Making the weaker argue   ment stronger." The truth, I suppose, they would not wish to state, namely, that it is become quite clear that they pretend to knowledge and know nothing. And because they are concerned for their pride, I think, and zealous, and numerous, and speak vehemently and persuasively about me, they have long filled your ears with zealous slander. It was on the strength of this that Meletus attacked me, along with Anytus and Lycon—Meletus angered on behalf of the poets, Anytus on behalf of the public craftsmen and the politicians, Lycon on behalf of

24a the orators. So the result is, as I said to begin with, that I should be most surprised were I able to remove from you in this short time a slander which has grown so great. There, Gentlemen of Athens, you have the truth, and I have concealed or misrepresented nothing in speaking it, great or small. Yet I know quite well that it is just for this that I have become hated—which is in fact an indication of the truth of what I say, and that this is the basis of the slander and charges against

b   me. Whether you inquire into it now or hereafter you will find it to be so.

REFUTATION OF MELETUS

Against the charges lodged by my first accusers, let this defense suffice. But for Meletus—the good man who loves his City, so he says—and for my later accusers, I shall attempt a further defense. Once more then, as before a different set of accusers, let us take up their sworn indictment.[8] It runs something like this: it says that Socrates is guilty of corrupting the youth, and of not acknowledging the gods the City acknowl-

c   edges, but other new divinities. Such is the charge. Let us examine its particulars.

It claims I am guilty of corrupting the youth. But I claim, Gentlemen of Athens, that it is Meletus who is guilty—guilty of jesting in earnest, guilty of lightly bringing men to trial, guilty of pretending a zealous concern for things he never cared about at all. I shall try to show you that this is true.

Come here, Meletus. Now tell me. Do you count it of great

d   importance that the young should be as good as possible?
"I do."

Then come and tell the jurors this: who improves them? Clearly you know, since it is a matter of concern to you.[9]

Having discovered, so you say, that I am the man who is corrupting them, you bring me before these judges to accuse me. But now come and say who makes them better. Inform the judges who he is.

You see, Meletus. You are silent. You cannot say. And yet, does this not seem shameful to you, and a sufficient indication of what I say, namely, that you never cared at all? Tell us, my friend. Who improves them?

"The laws."

e   But I did not ask you that, dear friend. I asked you what man improves them—whoever it is who in the first place knows just that very thing, the laws.

"These men, Socrates. The judges."

Really Meletus? These men here are able to educate the youth and improve them?

"Especially they."

All of them? Or only some?

"All."

By Hera, you bring good news. An ungrudging plenty of
25a   benefactors! But what about the audience here. Do they improve them, or not?

"They too."

And members of the Council?

"The Councillors too."

Well then Meletus, do the members of the Assembly, the Ecclesiasts, corrupt the young? Or do they all improve them too?

"They too."

So it seems that every Athenian makes them excellent except me, and I alone corrupt them. Is that what you are saying?

"That is exactly what I am saying."

You condemn me to great misfortune. But tell me, do you
b   think it is so with horses? Do all men improve them, while some one man corrupts them? Or quite to the contrary, is it some one man or a very few, namely horse-trainers, who are able to improve them, while the majority of people, if they handle horses and use them, corrupt them? Is that not true, Meletus, both of horses and all other animals? Of course it is, whether you and Anytus affirm or deny it. It would be good fortune indeed for the youth if only one man corrupted them and the rest benefited. But the fact is, Meletus, that you suffi-

c   ciently show that you never gave thought to the youth; you clearly indicate your own lack of concern, indicate that you never cared at all about the matters in which you bring action against me.

But again, dear Meletus, tell us this: is it better to dwell among fellow citizens who are good, or wicked? Do answer, dear friend; surely I ask nothing hard. Do not wicked men do evil things to those around them, and good men good things?

"Of course."

d   Now, is there anyone who wishes to be harmed rather than benefited by those with whom he associates? Answer me, dear friend, for the law requires you to answer. Is there anyone who wishes to be harmed?

"Of course not."

Very well then, are you bringing action against me here because I corrupt the youth intentionally, or unintentionally?

"Intentionally, I say."

How can that be, Meletus? Are you at your age so much wiser than I at mine that you recognize that evil men always

e   do evil things to those around them, and good men do good, while I have reached such a pitch of folly that I am unaware that if I do some evil to those with whom I associate, I shall very likely receive some evil at their hands, with the result that I do such great evil intentionally, as you claim? I do not believe you, Meletus, and I do not think anyone else does either. On the contrary: either I do not corrupt the youth, or

26a   if I do, I do so unintentionally. In either case, you lie. And if I corrupt them unintentionally, it is not the law to bring action here for that sort of mistake, but rather to instruct and admonish in private; for clearly, if I once learn, I shall stop what I unintentionally do. You, however, were unwilling to associate with me and teach me; instead, you brought action here, where it is law to bring those in need of punishment rather than instruction.

Gentlemen of Athens, what I said is surely now clear: Mel-

b   etus was never concerned about these matters, much or little. Still, Meletus, tell us this: how do you say I corrupt the youth? Or is it clear from your indictment that I teach them not to acknowledge gods the City acknowledges, but other new divinities? Is this what you mean by saying I corrupt by teaching?

"Certainly. That is exactly what I mean."

Then in the name of these same gods we are now discussing, Meletus, please speak a little more plainly still, both for me and for these gentlemen here. Do you mean that I teach the youth to acknowledge that there are gods, and thus do not myself wholly deny gods, and am not in that respect guilty—though the gods are not those the City acknowledges, but different ones? Or are you claiming that I do not myself acknowledge any gods at all, and teach this to others?

"I mean that. You acknowledge no gods at all."

Ah, my dear Meletus, why do you say such things? Do I not at least acknowledge Sun and Moon as gods, as other men do?

"No, no, Gentlemen and Judges, not when he says the Sun is a stone and the Moon earth."

My dear Meletus! Do you think it is Anaxagoras you are accusing?[10] Do you so despise these judges here and think them so unlettered that they do not know it is the books of Anaxagoras of Clazomenae which teem with such statements? Are young men to learn these things specifically from me, when they can buy them sometimes in the Orchestra[11] for a drachma, if the price is high, and laugh at Socrates if he pretends they are his own—especially since they are so absurd? Well, dear friend, is that what you think? I acknowledge no gods at all?

"No, none whatever."

You cannot be believed, Meletus—even, I think, by yourself. Gentlemen of Athens, I think this man who stands here before you is insolent and unchastened, and has brought this suit precisely out of insolence and unchastened youth. He seems to be conducting a test by propounding a riddle: "Will Socrates, the wise man, realize how neatly I contradict myself, or will I deceive him and the rest of the audience?" For certainly it seems clear that he is contradicting himself in his indictment. It is as though he were saying, "Socrates is guilty of not acknowledging gods, and acknowledges gods." Yet surely this is to jest.

Please join me, Gentlemen, in examining why it appears to me that this is what he is saying. And you answer us, Meletus. The rest of you will please remember what I asked you at the beginning, and make no disturbance if I fashion arguments in my accustomed way.

Is there any man, Meletus, who acknowledges that there are things pertaining to men, but does not acknowledge that there are men? Let him answer for himself, Gentlemen—and let him stop interrupting. Is there any man who does not acknowledge that there are horses, but acknowledges things pertaining to horsemanship? Or does not acknowledge that there are flutes, but acknowledges things pertaining to flute playing? There is not, my good friend. If you do not wish to answer, I'll answer for you and for the rest of these people here. But do please answer my next question, at least: Is there any man who

c   acknowledges that there are things pertaining to divinities, but does not acknowledge that there are divinities?

"There is not."

How obliging of you to answer—reluctantly, and under compulsion from these gentlemen here. Now, you say that I acknowledge and teach things pertaining to divinities—whether new or old, still at least I acknowledge them, by your account; indeed, you swore to that in your indictment. But if I acknowledge that there are things pertaining to divinities, must I surely not also acknowledge that there are divinities? Isn't that so? Of course it is—since you do not answer, I count you

d   as agreeing. And divinities, we surely believe, are either gods or children of gods? Correct?

"Of course."

So if I believe in divinities, as you say, and if divinities are a kind of god, there is the jesting riddle I attributed to you: you are saying that I do not believe in gods, and again that I do believe in gods because I believe in divinities. On the other hand, if divinities are children of gods, some born illegitimately of nymphs,[12] or others of whom this is also told,[13] who could

e   possibly believe that there are children of gods, but not gods? It would be as absurd as believing that there are children of horses and asses, namely, mules, without believing there are horses and asses. Meletus, you could not have brought this indictment except in an attempt to test us—or because you were at a loss for any true basis of prosecution. But as to how you are to convince anyone of even the slightest intelligence that one and the same man can believe that there are things

28a   pertaining to divinities and gods, and yet believe that there are neither divinities nor heroes—there is no way.

DIGRESSION: SOCRATES' MISSION TO ATHENS

Gentlemen of Athens, I do not think further defense is needed to show that, by the very terms of Meletus' indictment,

I am not guilty; this, surely, is sufficient. But as I said before, a great deal of enmity has risen against me among many people, and you may rest assured this is true. And that is what will convict me, if I am convicted—not Meletus, not Anytus,

b   but the grudging slander of the multitude. It has convicted many another good and decent man; I think it will convict me; nor is there reason to fear that with me it will come to a stand.

Perhaps someone may say, "Are you not ashamed, Socrates, at having pursued such a course that you now stand in danger of being put to death?" To him I would make a just reply: You are wrong, Sir, if you think that a man worth anything at all should take thought for danger in living or dying. He should look when he acts to one thing: whether what he does is just or unjust, the work of a good man or a bad one. By your ac-

c   count, those demigods and heroes who laid down their lives at Troy would be of little worth—the rest of them, and the son of Thetis[14] too; Achilles so much despised danger instead of submitting to disgrace that when he was intent on killing Hector his goddess mother told him, as I recall, "My son, if you avenge the slaying of your comrade Patroclus with the death of Hector, you yourself shall die; for straightway with Hector is his fate prepared for you."[15] Achilles heard, and thought little of the death and danger. He was more afraid to

d   live as a bad man, with friends left unavenged. "Straightway let me die," he said, "exacting right from him who did the wrong, that I may not remain here as a butt of mockery beside the crook-beaked ships, a burden to the earth." Do you suppose that he gave thought to death and danger?

Gentlemen of Athens, truly it is so: wherever a man stations himself in belief that it is best, wherever he is stationed by his commander, there he must I think remain and run the risks, giving thought to neither death nor any other thing except disgrace. I should indeed have wrought a fearful thing, Gentlemen of Athens, if, when the commanders you chose

e   stationed me at Potidaea and Amphipolis and Delium,[16] I there remained as others did, and ran the risk of death; but then, when the God stationed me, as I thought and believed, obliging me to live in the pursuit of wisdom, examining my-

29a   self and others—if then, at that point, through fear of death or any other thing, I left my post. That would have been dreadful indeed, and then in truth might I be justly brought to court for not acknowledging the existence of gods, for willful disobedience to the oracle, for fearing death, for thinking myself wise when I am not.

For to fear death, Gentlemen, is nothing but to think one is wise when one is not; for it is to think one knows what one does not. No man knows death, nor whether it is not the greatest of all goods; and yet men fear it as though they well

b   knew it to be the worst of evils. Yet how is this not folly most to be reproached, the folly of believing one knows what one does not? I, at least, Gentlemen, am perhaps superior to most men here and just in this, and if I were to claim to be wiser than anyone else it would be in this: that as I have no satisfactory knowledge of things in the Place of the Dead, I do not think I do. I do know that to be guilty of disobedience to a superior, be he god or man, is shameful evil.

So as against evils I know to be evils, I shall never fear or flee from things which for aught I know may be good. Thus,

c   even if you now dismiss me, refusing to do as Anytus bids— Anytus, who said that either I should not have been brought to trial to begin with or, since brought, must be put to death, testifying before you that if I were once acquitted your sons would pursue what Socrates teaches and all be thoroughly corrupted—if with this in view you were to say to me, "Socrates, we shall not at this time be persuaded by Meletus, and we dismiss you. But on this condition: that you no longer pass time in that inquiry of yours, or pursue philosophy. And

d   if you are again taken doing it, you die." If, as I say, you were to dismiss me on that condition, I would reply that I hold you in friendship and regard, Gentlemen of Athens, but I shall obey the God rather than you, and while I have breath and am able I shall not cease to pursue wisdom or to exhort you, charging any of you I happen to meet in my accustomed manner. "You are the best of men, being an Athenian, citizen of a city honored for wisdom and power beyond all others. Are you then not ashamed to care for the getting of money, and

e   reputation, and public honor, while yet having no thought or concern for truth and understanding and the greatest possible excellence of your soul?" And if some one of you disputes this, and says he does care, I shall not immediately dismiss him and go away. I shall question him and examine him and

30a   test him, and if he does not seem to me to possess virtue, and yet says he does, I shall rebuke him for counting of more importance things which by comparison are worthless. I shall do this to young and old, citizen and stranger, whomever I happen to meet, but I shall do it especially to citizens, in as much as they are more nearly related to me. For the God commands this, be well assured, and I believe that you have yet to gain in this City a greater good than my service to the God. I go about doing nothing but persuading you, young and old, to

b   care not for body or money in place of, or so much as, excellence of soul. I tell you that virtue does not come from money, but money and all other human goods both public and private from virtue. If in saying this I corrupt the youth, that would be harm indeed. But anyone who claims I say other than this speaks falsehood. In these matters, Gentlemen of Athens, be-

c   lieve Anytus, or do not. Dismiss me, or do not. For I will not do otherwise, even if I am to die for it many times over.

Please do not make a disturbance, Gentlemen. Abide in my request and do not interrupt what I have to say, but listen. Indeed, I think you will benefit by listening. I am going to tell you certain things at which you may perhaps cry out; please do not do it. Be well assured that if you kill me, and if I am the sort of man I claim, you will harm me less than you harm yourselves. There is no harm a Meletus or Anytus can do me; it is not possible, for it does not, I think, accord with divine law that a better man be harmed by a worse. Meletus perhaps

d   can kill me, or exile me, or disenfranchise me; and perhaps he and others too think those things great evils. I do not. I think it a far greater evil to do what he is now doing, attempting to kill a man unjustly. And so, Gentlemen of Athens, I am far from making a defense for my own sake, as some might think; I make it for yours, lest you mistake the gift the God has given you and cast your votes against me. If you kill me, you will not easily find such another man as I, a man who—if I may put it a bit absurdly—has been fastened as it were to the City by the God as to a large and well-bred horse, a horse grown sluggish because of its size, and in need of being roused by a kind of gadfly. Just so, I think, the God has fastened me to

31a the City. I rouse you. I persuade you. I upbraid you. I never stop lighting on each one of you, everywhere, all day long. Such another will not easily come to you again, Gentlemen, and if you are persuaded by me, you will spare me. But perhaps you are angry, as men roused from sleep are angry, and perhaps you will swat me, persuaded by Meletus that you may lightly kill. Then will you continue to sleep out your lives, unless the God sends someone else to look after you.

That I am just that, a gift from the God to the City, you
b   may recognize from this: it scarcely seems a human matter merely, that I should take no thought for anything of my own and endure the neglect of my house and its affairs for these long years now, and ever attend to yours, going to each of you in private like a father or elder brother, persuading you to care for virtue. If I got something from it, if I took pay for this kind of exhortation, that would explain it. But as things are, you can see for yourselves that even my accusers, who have accused me so shamefully of everything else, could not
c   summon shamelessness enough to provide witnesses to testify that I ever took pay or asked for it. For it is enough, I think, to provide my poverty as witness to the truth of what I say.

Perhaps it may seem peculiar that I go about in private advising men and busily inquiring, and yet do not enter your Assembly in public to advise the City. The reason is a thing you have heard me mention many times in many places, that something divine and godlike comes to me—which Meletus, indeed, mocked in his indictment.[17] I have had it from childhood. It comes as a kind of voice, and when it comes, it always turns me away from what I am about to do, but never toward it. That is what opposed my entering political life, and I think it did well to oppose. For be well assured, Gentlemen of Athens, that had I attempted long since to enter polit-
e   ical affairs, I should long since have been destroyed—to the benefit of neither you nor myself.

Please do not be angry at me for telling the simple truth. It is impossible for any man to be spared if he legitimately opposes you or any other democratic majority, and prevents
32a   many unjust and illegal things from occurring in his city. He who intends to fight for what is just, if he is to be spared even for a little time, must of necessity live a private rather than a public life.

I shall offer you a convincing indication of this—not words, but what you respect, deeds. Hear, then, what befell me, so that you may know that I will not through fear of death give way to any man contrary to what is right, even if I am destroyed for it. I shall tell you a thing which is tedious—it b   smacks of the law courts—but true. Gentlemen of Athens, I never held other office in the City, but I was once a member of the Council.[18] And it happened that our Tribe,[19] Antiochis, held the Prytanate[20] when you decided to judge as a group the cases of the ten generals who had failed to gather up the bodies of the slain in the naval battle,[21]—illegally, as later it seemed to all of you. But at the time, I alone of the Prytanies opposed doing a thing contrary to law, and cast my vote against it. And when the orators were ready to impeach me

c   and have me arrested—you urging them on with your shouts— I thought that with law and justice on my side I must run the risk, rather than concur with you in an unjust decision through fear of bonds or death. Those things happened while the City was still under the Democracy. But when Oligarchy came, the Thirty in turn summoned me along with four others to the Rotunda and ordered us to bring back Leon the Salamanian from Salamis so that he might be executed, just as they ordered many others to do such things, planning to implicate as many

d   people as possible in their own guilt. But I then showed again, not by words but deeds, that death, if I may be rather blunt, was of no concern whatever to me; to do nothing unjust or unholy—that was my concern. Strong as it was, that oligarchy did not so frighten me as to do a thing unjust, and when we departed the Rotunda, the other four went into Salamis and brought back Leon, and I left and went home. I might have been killed for that, if the oligarchy had not shortly afterward

e   been overthrown. And of these things you will have many witnesses.

     Now, do you think I would have lived so many years if I had been in public life and acted in a manner worthy of a good man, defending what is just and counting it, as is necessary, of first importance? Far from it, Gentlemen of Athens. Not I, and not any other man. But through my whole life I

33a   have shown myself to be that sort of man in public affairs, the few I've engaged in; and I have shown myself the same man in private. I never gave way to anyone contrary to what is just— not to others, and certainly not to those slanderously said to be my pupils. In fact, I have never been teacher to anyone. If, in speaking and tending my own affairs, anyone wished to hear me, young or old, I never begrudged him; nor do I dis-

b   cuss for a fee and not otherwise. To rich and poor alike I offer myself as a questioner, and if anyone wishes to answer, he may hear what I have to say. And if any of them turned out to be useful men, or any did not, I cannot justly be held responsible. To none did I promise instruction, and none did I teach; if anyone says that he learned from me or heard in private what others did not, you may rest assured he is not telling the truth.

c   Why is it, then, that some people enjoy spending so much time with me? You have heard, Gentlemen of Athens: I told you the whole truth. It is because they enjoy hearing people tested who think they are wise and are not. After all, it is not unamusing. But for my own part, as I say, I have been ordered to do this by God—in oracles, in dreams, in every way in which other divine apportionment ever ordered a man to do anything.

d   These things, Gentlemen of Athens, are both true and easily tested. For if I am corrupting some of the youth, and have corrupted others, it must surely be that some among them, grown older, if they realize that I counseled them toward evil while young, would now come forward to accuse me and exact a penalty. And if they were unwilling, then some of their relatives—fathers, brothers, other kinsmen—if their own relatives had suffered evil at my hands, would now remember, and exact a penalty. Certainly there are many such men I see present. Here is Crito, first, of my own age and deme,[22] father of Critobulus; then there is Lysanias of Sphettos, father of Aeschines[23] here. Next there is Antiphon of Cephisus, father of Epigenes. Then there are others whose brothers engaged in this pastime. There is Nicostratus, son of Theozotides, brother of Theodotus—and Theodotus is dead, so he could not have swayed him—and Paralus here, son of De-

34a   modocus, whose brother was Theages. And here is Adeimantus, son of Ariston, whose brother is Plato there; and Aeantodorus, whose brother is Apollodorus here. I could name many others, some of whom at least Meletus ought certainly have provided in his speech as witnesses. If he forgot it then, let him do it now—I yield the floor—and let him say whether he has any witnesses of the sort. You will find that quite to the contrary, Gentlemen, every one of these men is ready to help me—I, who corrupt their relatives, as Meletus and Anytus claim.

b   Those who are themselves corrupted might perhaps have reason to help me; but their relatives are older men who have not been corrupted. What reason could they have for supporting me except that it is right and just, because they know Meletus is lying and I am telling the truth?

Very well then, Gentlemen. This, and perhaps a few other things like it, is what I have to say in my defense. Perhaps
c   some of you will remember his own conduct and be offended, if when brought to trial on a lesser charge than this, he begged his judges with tearful supplication, and caused his children to come forward so that he might be the more pitied, along with other relatives and a host of friends; whereas I shall do none of these things, even though I am, as it would seem at least, in the extremity of danger. Perhaps someone with this in mind may become hardened against me; angered by it, he may cast
d   his vote in anger. If this is true of any of you—not that I expect it, but if it is—I think it might be appropriate to say, "I too have relatives, my friend; for as Homer puts it, I am not 'of oak and rock,' but born of man, so I have relatives—yes, and sons too, Gentlemen of Athens, three of them, one already a lad and two of them children. Yet not one of them have I caused to come forward here, and I shall not beg you to acquit me." Why not? Not out of stubbornness, Gentle-
e   men of Athens, nor disrespect for you. Whether or not I am confident in the face of death is another story; but I think that my own honor, and yours, and that of the whole City would suffer, if I were to behave in this way, I being of the age I am and having the name I have—truly or falsely, it being
35a   thought that Socrates is in some way superior to most men. If those of you reputed to be superior in wisdom or courage or any other virtue whatever are to be men of this sort, it would be disgraceful; I have often seen such people behave surprisingly when put on trial, even though they had a reputation to uphold, because they were persuaded that they would suffer a terrible thing if they were put to death—as though they would be immortal if you did not kill them. I think they cloak the City in shame, so that a stranger might think that those among the Athenians who are superior in vir-
b   tue, and whom the Athenians themselves judge worthy of office and other honors, are no better than women. These are things, Gentlemen of Athens, which those of you who have

a reputation to uphold ought not to do; nor if we defendants do them, ought you permit it. You ought rather make it clear that you would far rather cast your vote against a man who stages these pitiful scenes, and makes the City a butt of mockery, than against a man who shows quiet restraint.

c   But apart from the matter of reputation, Gentlemen, it does not seem to me just to beg a judge, or to be acquitted by begging; it is rather just to teach and persuade. The judge does not sit to grant justice as a favor, but to render judgment; he has sworn no oath to gratify those whom he sees fit, but to judge according to law. We ought not accustom you, nor ought you become accustomed, to forswear yourselves; it is pious in neither of us. So do not expect me, Gentlemen of Athens, to do such things in your presence as I believe to be

d   neither honorable nor just nor holy, especially since, by Zeus, it is for impiety that I am being prosecuted by this fellow Meletus here. For clearly, if I were to persuade and compel you by supplication, you being sworn as judges, I would teach you then indeed not to believe that there are gods, and in making my defense I would in effect accuse myself of not acknowledging them. But that is far from so; I do acknowledge them, Gentlemen of Athens, as no one of my accusers does, and to you and to the God I now commit my case, to judge in whatever way shall be best both for me and for you.

II. The Counterpenalty

e   I am not distressed, Gentlemen of Athens, at what has hap-
36a   pened, nor angered that you have cast your votes against me. Many things contribute to this, among them the fact that I expected it. I am much more surprised at the number of votes either way: I did not think it would be by so little, but by more. As it is, it seems, if only thirty votes had fallen otherwise, I would have been acquitted.[24] And so far as Meletus at least is concerned, it seems to me, I am already acquitted—and more than acquitted, since it is clear that if Anytus and Lycon had not come forward to accuse me, Meletus would have been

b   fined a thousand drachmas for not obtaining a fifth part of the vote.[25]

The man demands death for me. Very well. Then what counterpenalty shall I propose to you, Gentlemen of Athens?[26]

Clearly something I deserve, but what? What do I deserve to pay or suffer because I did not through life keep quiet, and yet did not concern myself, as the multitude do, with money or property or military and public honors and other office, or the secret societies and political clubs which keep cropping

c   up in the City, believing that I was really too reasonable and temperate a man to enter upon these things and survive. I did not go where I could benefit neither you nor myself; instead, I went to each of you in private, where I might perform the greatest service. I undertook to persuade each of you not to care for any thing which belongs to you before first caring for yourselves, nor to care for anything which belongs to the City before caring for the City itself, and so too with everything

d   else. Now, what do I deserve to suffer for being this sort of man? Some good thing, Gentlemen of Athen, if penalty is really to be assessed according to desert. What then is fitting for a poor man who has served his City well, and needs leisure to exhort you? Why, Gentlemen of Athens, nothing is more fitting for such a man than to be fed in the Prytaneum, at the common table of the City—yes, and far more fitting than for one of you who has been an Olympic victor in the single-horse or two- or four-horse chariot races.[27] For he makes you seem happy, whereas I make you happy in truth, and he does not

e   need subsistence,[28] and I do. If then I must propose a penalty

37a   I justly deserve, I propose that, public subsistence in the Prytaneum.

Perhaps some of you will think that in saying this I speak much as I spoke of tears and pleading, out of stubborn pride. That is not so, Gentlemen of Athens, though something of this sort is: I am persuaded that I have not intentionally wronged any man, but I cannot persuade you of it; we have talked so short a time. Now, I believe if you had a law, as

b   other people do, that cases involving death shall not be decided in a single day, that you would be persuaded; but as things are, it is not easy in so short a time to do away with slanders grown so great. Being persuaded, however, that I have wronged no one, I am quite unwilling to wrong myself, or claim that I deserve some evil and propose any penalty of the kind. What is there to fear? That I may suffer the penalty Meletus proposes, when as I say, I do not know whether it is good or evil? Shall I choose instead a penalty I know very well to be evil?

Imprisonment, perhaps? But why should I live in prison, a
c   slave to men who happen to occupy office as the Eleven?[29] A
fine, then, and imprisonment till I pay it? But that comes to
the same thing, since I have no money to pay it. Shall I then
propose exile? Perhaps you would accept that. But I must indeed love life and cling to it dearly, Gentlemen, if I were so
d   foolish as to think that, although you, my own fellow-citizens,
cannot bear my pursuits and discussions, which have become
so burdensome and hateful that you now seek to be rid of
them, others will bear them lightly. No, Gentlemen. My life
would be fine indeed, if at my age I went to live in exile, always moving from city to city, always driven out. For be well
assured that wherever I go, the young men will listen to what
I say as they do here; if I turn them away they will themselves
e   drive me out, appealing to their elders; if I do not turn them
away, their fathers and relations will drive me out in their behalf.

Perhaps someone may say, "Would it not be possible for
you to live in exile, Socrates, if you were silent and kept
quiet?" But this is the hardest thing of all to make some of
you believe. If I say that to do so would be to disobey the
38a   God, and therefore I cannot do it, you will not believe me because you will think that I am being sly and dishonest.[30] If on
the other hand I say that the greatest good for man is to fashion arguments each day about virtue and the other things you
hear me discussing, when I examine myself and others, and
that the unexamined life is not for man worth living, you will
believe what I say still less. I claim these things are so, Gentlemen; but it is not easy to convince you. At the same time, I
b   am not accustomed to think myself deserving of any evil. If I
had money, I would propose a fine as great as I could pay—
there would be no harm in that. But as things stand, I have
no money, unless the amount I can pay is the amount you are
willing to exact of me. I might perhaps be able to pay a mina
of silver.[31] So I propose a penalty in that amount. But Plato
here, Gentlemen of Athens, and Crito and Critobulus and
Apollodorus bid me propose thirty minas, and they will stand
surety. So I propose that amount. You have guarantors sufficient for the sum.

III. Epilogue

c   For the sake of only a little time, Gentlemen of Athens, you are to be accused by those who wish to revile the City of having killed Socrates, a wise man—for those who wish to reproach you will say I am wise even if I am not. And if you had only waited a little, the thing would have come of its own initiative. You see my age. You see how far spent my life already is, how near to death.

d   I say this, not to all of you, but to those of you who voted to condemn me. To them I also say this. Perhaps you think, Gentlemen of Athens, that I have been convicted for lack of words to persuade you, had I thought it right to do and say anything to be acquitted. Not so. It is true I have been convicted for a lack; not a lack of words, but lack of bold shamelessness, unwillingness to say the things you would find it pleasant to hear—weeping and wailing, saying and doing many

e   things I claim to be unworthy of me, but things of the sort you are accustomed to hear from others. I did not then think it necessary to do anything unworthy of a free man because of danger; I do not now regret so having conducted my defense; and I would far rather die with that defense than live with the other. Neither in court of law nor in war ought I or any man contrive to escape death by any means possible.

39a   Often in battle it becomes clear that a man may escape death by throwing down his arms and turning in supplication to his pursuers; and there are many other devices for each of war's dangers, so that one can avoid dying if he is bold enough to say and do anything at all. It is not difficult to escape death, Gentlemen; it is more difficult to escape wickedness, for wick-

b   edness runs faster than death. And now I am old and slow, and I have been caught by the slower runner. But my accusers are clever and quick, and they have been caught by the faster runner, namely Evil. I now take my leave, sentenced by you to death; they depart convicted by Truth for injustice and wickedness. I abide in my penalty, and they in theirs. That is no doubt as it should be, and I think it is fit.

c   I desire next to prophesy to you who condemned me. For I have now reached that point where men are especially prophetic, when they are about to die. I say to you who have decreed my death that to you there will come hard on my dying a thing far more difficult to bear than the death you have visited upon me. You have done this thing in the belief that you would be released from submitting to examination in your lives. I say that it will turn out otherwise. Those who

d   come to examine you will be more numerous, and I have up to now restrained them, though you perceived it not. They will be more harsh inasmuch as they are younger, and you will be the more troubled. If you think by killing to hold back the reproach due you for not living rightly, you are profoundly mistaken. That release is neither possible nor honorable. The release which is both most honorable and most easy is not to cut down others, but to so prepare yourselves that you will be as good as possible. This I utter as prophecy to you who voted for my condemnation, and take my leave.[32]

e   But with you who voted for my acquittal, I should be glad to discuss the nature of what has happened, now, while the authorities are busy and I am not yet gone where, going, I must die. Abide with me, Gentlemen, this space of time; nothing prevents our talking with each other while we still can.

40a   To you, as my friends, I wish to display the meaning of what has now fallen to my lot. A remarkable thing has occurred, Gentlemen and Judges—and I am correct in calling you Judges. My accustomed oracle, which is divine,[33] always came quite frequently before in everything, opposing me even in trivial matters if I was about to err. And now a thing has fallen to my lot which you also see yourselves, a thing which some might think, and do in fact believe, to be ultimate among evils. But the sign of the God did not oppose me early this morning

b   when I left my house, nor when I came up to the court room here, nor at any point in my argument in anything I was about to say. And yet in many places, in other arguments, it has checked me right in the middle of speaking; but today it has not opposed me in any way, in none of my deeds, in none of my words. What do I take to be the reason? I will tell you. Very likely what has fallen to me is good, and those among

c   us who think that death is an evil are wrong. There has been convincing indication of this. For the accustomed sign would surely have opposed me, if I were not in some way acting for good.

Let us also consider a further reason for high hope that death is good. Death is one of two things. Either to be dead is not to exist, to have no awareness at all, or it is, as the stories tell, a kind of alteration, a change of abode for the soul from this place to another. And if it is to have no awareness, like a

d   sleep when the sleeper sees no dream, death would be a wonderful gain; for I suppose if someone had to pick out that night in which he slept and saw no dream, and put the other days and nights of his life beside it, and had to say after inspecting them how many days and nights he had lived in his life which were better and sweeter, I think that not only any ordinary person but even the Great King[34] himself would find them easily numbered in relation to other days, and other

e   nights. If death is that, I say it is gain; for the whole of time then turns out to last no longer than a single night. But if on the contrary death is like taking a journey, passing from here to another place, and the stories told are true, and all who have died are there—what greater good might there be, my Judges? For if a man once goes to the place of the dead, and takes leave of those who claim to be judges here, he will find

41 a   the true judges who are said to sit in judgment there—Minos, Rhadamanthus, Aeacus, Triptolemus, and the other demigods and heroes who lived just lives. Would that journey be worthless? And again, to meet Orpheus and Musaeus, Hesiod and Homer—how much would any of you give? I at least would be willing to die many times over, if these things are true. I

b   would find a wonderful pursuit there, when I met Palamedes, and Ajax, son of Telemon, and any others among the ancients done to death by unjust verdicts, and compared my experiences with theirs. It would not, I think, be unamusing. But the greatest thing, surely, would be to test and question there as I did here—who among them is wise? Who thinks he is and is not? How much might one give, my Judges, to examine the

c   man who led the great army against Troy,[35] or Odysseus, or Sisyphus, or a thousand other men and women one might mention—to converse with them, to associate with them, to examine them—why, it would be inconceivable happiness. Especially since they surely do not kill you for it there. For they are happier there than men are here in other ways, and they are already immortal for the rest of time, if the stories told are true.

But you too, my Judges, must be of good hope concerning death. You must recognize that this one thing is true: that d   there is no evil for a good man either in living or in dying, and that the gods do not neglect his affairs. What has now come to me did not come of its own initiative. It is clear to me that to die now and be released from my affairs is better for me. That is why the sign did not turn me back, and I bear no anger whatever toward those who voted to condemn me, or toward my accusers. And yet, it was not with this in mind

e   that they accused and convicted me. They thought to do harm, and for that they deserve blame. But this much would I ask of them: when my sons are grown, Gentlemen, exact a penalty of them: give pain to them exactly as I gave pain to you, if it seems to you that they care more for wealth or anything else than they care for virtue. And if they seem to be something and are nothing, rebuke them as I rebuked you, because they do not care for what they ought, because they think themselves something and are worth nothing. And should you do

42a   that, both I and my sons will have been justly dealt with at your hands.

But it is already the hour of parting—I to die and you to live. Which of us goes to the better is unclear to all but the God.

The Crito

Analysis

The *Crito* is a companion dialogue to the *Apology*. Its level of thought and expression are characteristically Platonic; but the style is sometimes copious to the point of repetition, and the thought turns on a dialogue within the dialogue, between Socrates and the Laws of Athens, which consists largely in rhetoric and has often been dismissed as 'myth'. It is not perhaps surprising that the *Crito* has often been treated, not as a philosophical argument, but as a document in the biography of Socrates, an exhibition of his strength of character in the face of death.

But rhetoric, if it is not philosophy, is an instrument by which philosophy is served, as the *Apology* does not state but shows, and the issues involved in this particular specimen of rhetoric are of some interest. Socrates, lying in prison awaiting execution, is presented with an opportunity to escape. He chooses instead to go to his death, giving as his reason that the law has decreed his execution, and that it is wrong to disobey the law. As a complicating factor in this decision, it is suggested that the specific application of law which requires his death is itself unjust, in that he was not guilty of the charge of impiety under which he lies condemned.

By any standards, this is a hard case, and one which raises a simple question. Can it conceivably be true—and one is entitled to suspect that those critics who have praised Socrates' excellence of character to the neglect of his argument have thought it could not—that a man ought to abide by his own death sentence, given that the sentence was rendered according to law, and that he is not guilty?

The *Crito* is an early essay on a topic which was to occupy a large place in Plato's mind and energies for the remainder of his life, and it is tempting to look to what came later—the *Republic* and the *Laws*, for example—as more mature. But the dialogue stands as comment on a great fifth-century debate, conducted not only by sophists and dramatists but by plain men and politicians, on the nature of law and legal obligation. The debate gained added urgency in Athens not only from the moral issues raised by a draining and ultimately catastrophic war, but also by a series of continuing legal reforms begun some two hundred years before by Plato's own ancestor, Solon. Then, at the close of the fifth century, came radical democracy, oligarchical revolution, and restoration. Plato, when he wrote the *Crito*, was heir to a discussion, and had been spectator to a sequence of events, which in personal terms must have taken on new meaning in the wake of Socrates' trial and execution. If he was a young man when he wrote—he was, to be exact, somewhere in his thirties—he was also a philosopher of genius. It is worth observing in addition that the *Crito* probably represents the mind of the historical Socrates with some accuracy. It is likely that Socrates was offered an opportunity to escape.[1] If so, he refused. If he refused, he had reasons. If he had reasons, the *Crito* may be presumed to present them. Certainly if there is any merit in the analysis of the dialogue here offered, there is nothing immature about its argument, which is one of elegant and cogent beauty.

Introductory Conversation (43a-44b)

The scene is Socrates' prison cell, just before first light. Crito, an old and valued friend of Socrates' own age and deme, has come with news that Socrates' execution is imminent.

It has been nearly a month since the trial. Under Athenian law, men found guilty on a capital charge were ordinarily executed within a few days of trial, but an accident prolonged Socrates' life. He was tried the day after the priest of Apollo crowned the stern of the sacred ship which Athens sent each year to Delos, Apollo's major shrine, in thanksgiving to the God. While the ship was gone, the City was kept ritually clean, and no executions were performed (*Phaedo* 58a-c). On this occasion the ship was detained by contrary winds, and Socrates had to endure a fairly lengthy imprisonment—an unusual indignity for an

Athenian citizen. Crito and other friends had offered to stand surety against escape in order to obtain freedom for him during this time (see *Phaedo* 115d). Not surprisingly, since the conviction was capital, the request was denied.

The ancients did not have dreams, but saw them, and Socrates saw, late in the night, a beautiful woman clothed in white who prophesied to him. Dreams seen after midnight were likely to be true, and such a figure and the color of her clothing were signs of good fortune to come.[2] The dream confirms Socrates' belief, affirmed in the *Apology* (40a-c, 41d, cf. 29a-b), that there is reason to think death a good.

Exhortation to Escape (44b-46a)

But Socrates need not die. There is still time to escape, and Crito has made the necessary arrangements. He argues that Socrates will disgrace himself and his friends if he allows himself to be executed, and give comfort to his enemies in the bargain. He will also fail in the duty he owes his children, leaving them fatherless at an age when they need him. Escape, on the other hand, can be arranged without danger to friends, and if he goes into exile, there is a place for him in Thessaly, where he will be protected.

It is important to observe that Crito's plea to Socrates to escape is a specimen of rhetoric. The plea begins with and twice repeats the injunction, "Be thou persuaded by me," but the persuasion offered is, as the *Gorgias* puts it, "at random." Crito offers, not a sequential argument organized around a single principle, but a cluster of considerations which might have been put in any order, like the epitaph of Midas the Phyrgian.

Crito's plea begins, ends, and is mainly based on, "how things will look." It bespeaks the persistence of moral attitudes as old as Homer. Professor Dodds remarks:

Homeric man's highest good is not the enjoyment of a quiet conscience, but the enjoyment of *timē*, public esteem. . . . And the strongest moral force which Homeric man knows is not the fear of god, but respect for public opinion. . . . In such a society, anything which exposes a man to the contempt or ridicule of his fellows, which causes him to "lose face," is felt as unbearable.[3]

This very accurately describes a leading theme in Crito's plea; the pivot of his reasoning, to the degree that it has a pivot, turns on the connected concepts of shame and success. That is why he can mourn, in one and the same breath, two things which to many modern readers will seem simply incommensurable: the loss of such friendship as he shall not find again, and the disgrace of appearing to the Many to put money before friends (44b-c).

An index of the power of shame in molding Greek moral attitudes is offered by Aristotle:

Since shame is a mental picture of disgrace, in which we shrink from the disgrace itself, and not from its consequences, and we only care what opinion is held of us because of the people who form the opinion, it follows that the people before whom we feel shame are those whose opinion of us matters to us.[4]

Shame is external, in that a man's estimate of himself and his actions is a function of the estimate of other people, or of the community at large. The pull of that standard was so strong that Aristotle in the *Nicomachean Ethics* concluded that good men will never fear shame or disgrace, because they will not only abstain from what is wrong but from what is thought to be wrong:

The sense of disgrace is not even characteristic of a good man, since it is consequent on bad actions (for such actions should not be done; and if some actions are disgraceful in very truth and others only according to common opinion, this makes no difference; for neither class of action should be done, so that no disgrace should be felt); and it is a mark of a bad man even to be such as to do any disgraceful action.[5]

Crito's preoccupation with shame and disgrace is not to be dismissed as accidental or idiosyncratic. It conforms to deeply rooted Greek moral attitudes.

There is a further element in Crito's plea. That death is well avoided (44d) is a reason for escape. That a father owes a duty to his children (45c-d) is a reason for escape. That friends need not be harmed by it (44e-45a) is a reason for not refusing to escape. But why, after all, does Crito as a reasonable man suppose that it is somehow more shameful to be convicted of a crime and executed than to be convicted of a crime and escape? Why does he think that if Socrates refuses to escape and goes to his death instead, he will be 'bad' and 'cowardly' or 'unmanly' (45e-46a)? Where is there cowardice or unmanliness in a death like that? And why should Crito himself feel disgrace at not having engineered a jail-break (44c)?

The reason is that, to an important degree, traditional Greek morality was a success morality. The good man is typically the man who wins. This theme of popular morals is repeatedly exhibited in the early and middle dialogues. Meno defines the excellence of a man as, "managing the affairs of his city, and so managing them as to work good to his friends and harm to his enemies, taking care to avoid such things himself" (*Meno* 71e). So too, Polemarchus thinks that justice is bene- fiting friends and harming enemies (*Republic* I 334b). The good man succeeds, and helps his friends. The bad man fails, and in his failure becomes disgraced; he is unmanly as having fallen short of the stan- dard of performance that a man, to be a man, must attain—a failure which may be involuntary, and yet issue in blame. To be convicted of a crime is to fail, and be disgraced, in a rather conspicuous way; to be executed for it when one might escape is to carry failure further. It is, as Crito puts it (45a), "to speed such a thing for yourself as your very enemies might speed for you," and in a society in which no one had ever suggested that you must love your enemies or do good to those who curse you, the triumph of adversaries was an evil keenly felt (see *Apology* 39a-b). If to fail is to be disgraced, then of all failures execu- tion as a common criminal is most disgraceful, and in the Athens of Socrates, as in the Athens of Saint Paul, such death was not regarded as a likely prelude to transfiguration.

Crito stands as an advocate, pleading a cause to his friend on be- half of his friend, using, as a pleader will, such terms as he can muster to persuade. If those terms exhibit one side of Greek popular morality —a side which if now differently phrased remains still part of our own—it is to be recalled that popular morality is not composed of a self-consistent set of principles. Ancient and modern, men value suc- cess and fear shame, place weight on competitive goods and the es- teem of their fellows. But precisely because, in order to live, they must live with each other, they also value cooperation and harmony, the virtues of justice and temperance associated with lawfulness and law (*Gorgias* 504d). The randomness of Crito's persuasion answers to an underlying incoherence in his plea. If shame and success were the only elements operative in his moral universe, he would be unable to understand, let alone accept, the appeal which Socrates will make to justice and the excellence of the soul. Further, there is implicit incon- sistency, exposed in the *Gorgias*, in the plea itself. Shame and success may seem to go hand in hand—succeed, or be disgraced. But they do not present a coherent basis for judgment, because the man best able to satisfy the standard of success is precisely the tyrant, who may rule without shame. Thus it is that Callicles, who dares to say what many men believe but are ashamed to say, rejects the morality of ordinary social convention and the praise and blame that attend on it as fit only for slaves, and brings as a reproach against philosophy that it unfits a man to defend himself. It is a law of nature—a *nomos* of *physis*—that the strong should rule and oppress the weak.[6] Success, become power, has conquered shame. Callicles, it may be observed, is no sophist, but a well-educated young Athenian gentleman: it is not an accident that his words echo those of the Athenian emissaries in the Melian Dialogue.[7] Crito is a good and decent man, speaking the language of popular morals. But popular morality was many things, not one, and in its incoherence combined surface decency with sinister depths.

Socrates' Reply to Crito (46b-49a)

Socrates' reply to Crito epitomizes what F. M. Cornford once called, without apology to Copernicus or Kant, the Socratic Revolution. The reply is a transformation from outer to inner: shame becomes reverence for truth, success attainment of justice. As Callicles remarks in the *Gorgias* (481c), "Socrates, if you are serious and what you say is really true, our human life would be turned upside down; we are doing exactly the opposite, it seems, of what we should."

Whether or not Socrates should escape has nothing to do with what most people think, but solely with whether it is right or wrong, just or unjust (47c). That question must be settled by *logoi*, arguments, accounts, reasoned conclusions (47b). Moral authority rests, not with the Many, who act at random, but with "he who understands things just and unjust," that is, with the Truth itself (48a; see also 47d). If we look to Aristotle's remark that "the people before whom we feel shame are those whose opinion matters to us,"[8] then Socrates' reply to Crito consists in altering the term of the relation, transferring it from the Many who do not have moral knowledge to the one man who does. What is primary in this alteration is not, of course, the man but the knowledge, for the man with knowledge need not be other than ourselves. If shame we are to feel, then it is before Truth as discovered in reasoned arguments that shame should be felt (see 48c-d).

If Socrates alters the terms of shame, he also alters the meaning of success. He proceeds by analogy. If we disobey the judgment of those who know and understand—specifically, physicians and trainers—we shall ruin a possession of ours which is benefited by health and harmed by disease. This is the body. But—and, since this is a matter of past argument, Socrates assumes rather than argues the point—there is another possession of ours which is benefited by justice and harmed by injustice (47d-e), and which is to be explicitly contrasted with the body as being of higher worth (48a). This possession, though Socrates does not here give it a name, is the soul.

This argument is a version of what may be called the Socratic Proportion, that Health : Body :: Virtue : Soul.[9] With that proportion runs the corollary that as the relation of health to the body is a matter of knowledge, to be sought in the arts of the physician and trainer, so the relation of virtue to the soul is equally a matter of knowledge, to be sought in a thing which before had no name, but which Socrates identified as philosophy, the love of wisdom.

The bearing of all this on the question of escape is direct. It is not living, but living well, which is of more importance; and to live well is to live honorably and justly. Granting that the soul is of higher worth than the body, and that it is benefited by justice and harmed by injustice, the question of whether to escape reduces to the question of whether it is just or unjust to do so (48b-d, cf. *Apology* 29c-30c). That is equivalent to the question whether escape will benefit or harm the soul.

There is some faint element of paradox in a success standard which, once internalized, may require voluntary acceptance of execution on the part of the man who succeeds. Even so sensitive and convinced a Platonist as Samuel Clarke, who strenuously maintained as a self-evident truth akin to the truths of Euclid that virtue is good in itself, argued in his *Boyle Lectures* of 1705 that, "It is not truly reasonable that men by adhering to Virtue should part with their lives, if thereby they eternally deprive themselves of all possibility of receiving any advantage from that adherence."[10] Clarke of course did not mean that it is unreasonable for men by adhering to virtue to part with their lives; he thought it perfectly reasonable. He meant—and Kant, treating the matter as a truth of practical reason for which there is and can be no theoretical proof, was afterwards to agree—that virtue implies desert of reward as part of the eternal fitness of things, and that since virtue may on occasion lead men to death, the fitness of things requires immortality. This theorem has a converse. It is, after all, one of the most familiar and certain facts of life that, although the rain falls on both just and unjust, the just get wet because the unjust have stolen their umbrellas. Recognition of this great truth leads easily to the thought of an afterlife, in which future umbrellas shall be apportioned according to past desert. It may also lead those of more dour temperament to hope or believe that the umbrellas stolen by the fathers shall be visited upon the children even unto the seventh generation, and that they shall leak. Clearly, if virtue is to be rewarded solely because it is virtuous, vice should be punished solely because it is vicious. Though the wicked in this life may seem to flourish like the green bay tree, picturesque unpleasantness awaits.

The nexus of ideas is alien to the thought of the *Crito*. It is, of course, Platonic: the glowing assertion of immortality in the *Gorgias* and the *Phaedo* is accompanied by an eschatological myth. But nothing in the *Crito* turns on immortality, a subject about which Socrates in the *Apology* (40c-41c) is agnostic. Socrates' concern for the soul is concern for the soul in this life, concern for moral excellence in the here and now. Clarke to the contrary notwithstanding, Socrates thinks it is eminently reasonable to lay down life without expectation of future reward, if the alternative is to do injustice. The Socratic Proportion implies that, as health is not a means to the good of the body, but its proper excellence, so virtue is not a means to the good of the soul, but its proper excellence. Justice, if it is a virtue, an excellence, is not a mere means to an end, but itself constitutive of the true end of human life. And as we look to the arts of the physician and trainer in matters of health, so we must look to the wise man—the statesman and true rhetorician of the *Gorgias*—in matters of justice and virtue.

If justice has to do with the good of the soul, then the criterion for determining whether an action is right or wrong is benefit or harm to the soul. Given that harm to the soul is the worst of all harms, and that he who acts unjustly harms his own soul, we are led from the *Crito* to the *Gorgias*, and the paradox that it is better to suffer injustice than to do it.

Two Premises (49a-50a)

Socrates next proceeds to establish two premises, on which the remainder of the discussion will depend. These are the wrongfulness of returning injustice for injustice or injury for injury, and the rightfulness of abiding by agreements, given that they are just.

The premise that one must do things he agreed to do, given that they are just, is stated without argument and treated as obvious. Still, it requires some comment. The word translated 'agree' has the force of a promise; but 'promise' is an unsatisfactory translation, since the Greek suggests *mutual* assent. Again, it may be claimed that the premise is ambiguous: is it that one must do what he agreed if the agreement is just? Or that one must do what he agreed if to do so is just? But the two elements in the ambiguity are equivalent, since each implies the other: an agreement cannot be just if, in a given situation, to act according to it is not to act justly. The rider that things agreed to ought to be done *given that they are just* is important. Socrates does not suppose, as Kant was later to do, that the obligation to keep promises or abide by agreements is 'strict' or 'perfect', that once agreement has been entered, nothing can justify its breach. There may be circumstances in which one may justly refuse to abide by an agreement. The point is put clearly in the *Republic* (I 331c), in an argument which, since it can be glossed from Xenophon's *Memorabilia*, pretty clearly belonged to the historical Socrates: if a friend when sane left weapons in your keeping on your promise to return them, and having gone mad demands them back, it would not be just to return them, nor to speak only the truth to a person in that condition. This illustrates a general Socratic and Platonic attitude toward moral, as distinct from legal, rules: they have binding force only as justice requires.

We nowadays claim to attach great importance to promises: some promises, we say, are sacred, and the keeping of them involves faithfulness or fidelity. As a matter of moral psychology, the connection of sacredness and faith is not accidental: it derives from the historical association of promising with the oath or the vow—the oath of fealty, whose breach was felony, the vow sworn before God, whose breach imperiled the fate of the immortal soul. The emphasis on promise-keeping in contemporary positive morality is in large degree the effect of feudal Christianity: promise-keeping was not among those duties delivered to Israel on Sinai, and, apart from the Covenant between Jehovah and his people, occupies a rather less prominent place in the *Pentateuch* than the duty not to seethe the kid in its mother's milk; in a different culture, Plato and Aristotle, though they had much to say about justice and virtue, scarcely attend to promise-keeping at all.[11]

The sense of sacredness which in latter days has been attributed to promises does much to explain why Kant thought it sensible to propose promise-keeping as a duty of perfect obligation.[12] If the example of Kant is insufficiently current, J. L. Austin's analysis of promises as performatives offers ample instruction. Austin meant to sanitize promising of its spirituality—or more exactly, if we are to trust his description of it, of its sacramental quality. The Courts Christian could only have greeted the results with discreet sacerdotal applause:

We are apt to have a feeling that their (sc., such awe-inspiring performatives as promises) being serious consists in their being uttered as (merely) the outward and visible sign, for convenience or for information, of an inward and spiritual act: from which it is but a short step to go on to believe or to assume without realizing that for many purposes the outward utterance is a description, *true or false*, of the occurrence of the inward performance. The classic expression of this

idea is to be found in the *Hippolytus* (1.612), where Hippolytus says . . . "my
tongue swore to, but my heart (or mind or other backstage *artiste*) did not."
Thus "I promise to . . ." obliges me—puts on record my spiritual assumption of
a spiritual shackle. It is gratifying to observe in this very example how excess of
profundity, or rather solemnity, at once paves the way for immorality. For one
who says "promising is not merely an uttering of a word! It is an inward and
spiritual act!" is apt to appear as a solid moralist standing out against a generation of superficial theorizers: we see him as he sees himself, surveying the invisible depths of ethical space, with all the distinction of a specialist in the *sui
generis*. Yet he provides Hippolytus with a let-out, the bigamist with an excuse
for his "I do" and the welsher with a defense for his "I bet." Accuracy and morality alike are on the side of the plain saying that *our word is our bond*.[13]

The plain saying, of course, represents a rule of canon law, and if it is
difficult to refute the claim that anybody ever thought that promising
was a description of a mental act or state, it is equally difficult to suppose that anybody ever believed it. It is canonically right to welsh on
bets, because gambling is wrong and welshing discourages the practice:
welshing, indeed, conforms to the strictest standards of the Kantian
Categorical Imperative, since if everybody welshed, there would be
no gambling. And Hippolytus, except to a specialist in the *sui generis*,
has a defense.

Hippolytus, let us recall, was sworn to secrecy by a nurse, who
proceeded to tell him of the love of Phaedra, his father's wife, and his
stepmother. An eccentric youth much given to chastity and horses,
Hippolytus broke his promise to the nurse with the justification Austin quotes, and sent a letter to Phaedra upbraiding her. She thereupon
wrote another letter, accusing Hippolytus of having raped her, and
committed suicide. Theseus, Hippolytus' father, thereupon cursed
him. Hippolytus went horse racing, and was killed. In short, this is
Greek tragedy, and a good time was had by all.

Now, whatever one makes of the particular circumstances in which
Hippolytus acted, promise breaking was surely the least of his troubles.
Promising may involve unforeseen consequences which are no part of
the intent with which the promise is made; and when those consequences become evident, it may be permissible or even obligatory to
break the promise. There is a distinction, in short, between words of
promise, and the knowledge and intent involved in the promise; and
the latter element, it may be observed, is mental. Some promises, indeed, impose no obligation whatever: for example, promises to do
what is wrong, even though the wrong does not appear on the face of
the promise.

In short, it often makes perfectly good sense to say that though the tongue has sworn, the mind was unsworn, and accuracy and morality alike are on the side of saying that our word is not always our bond. Henry Sidgwick concluded that:

It appears that a clear *consensus* can only be claimed for the principle that a promise, express or tacit, is binding, if a number of conditions are fulfilled: viz. if the promiser has a clear belief as to the sense in which it was understood by the promisee, and if the latter is still in a position to grant release from it, but unwilling to do so, if it was not obtained by force or fraud, if it does not conflict with definite prior obligations, if we do not believe that its fulfillment will be harmful to the promisee, or will inflict a disproportionate sacrifice on the promiser, and if circumstances have not materially changed since it was made. If any of these conditions fails, the *consensus* seems to become evanescent, and the common moral perceptions of thoughtful persons fall into obscurity and disagreement.[14]

If the analysis of promises as performatives, that is, as speech-acts, implies that the duties of promise keeping are absolute, then that analysis is false to its subject matter.

In the concrete situation envisaged in the *Crito*, there is something eccentric—not to say repugnant—in the notion that the duties of promise keeping may of their own force obligate a man to accept an unjust sentence of death, and the source of the eccentricity is clear. It assumes that the existence of agreement is the sole ground for the justice of abiding by it, whereas in fact the justice of abiding by it is a condition for honoring the agreement. The qualification that things agreed to ought to be done given that they are just is crucial to the analysis of promising.

The premise that things agreed to are to be done when they are just is central to the argument of the Laws of Athens which is to follow. The Laws will maintain that Socrates, by continuing to live as a citizen, has entered an implied agreement to abide by the decisions of courts. They will also allow that the particular verdict under which Socrates lies condemned may well be unjust, in that he is innocent of the charge of which he was found guilty. If this is so, it is an easy inference that the binding claim of agreement has been loosed: when a man signs on to sail on the ship of state, he does not thereby contract to be thrown overboard at the whim of the other passengers, and there is no apparent justice in abiding by agreements which carry the consequence of innocent death. But it will be found that agreement is not used to provide an independent reason for refusing to escape. Rather, it establishes the authority of law over Socrates as a citizen.

The wrongfulness of escape will be found to consist, not in breach of agreement, but in the fact that such breach implies injury to the legal order, the Laws of Athens, by denial of its authority. In short, the wrongfulness of escape derives from the primacy of justice.

One must never do injustice—the *must* here, as in English, is equivalent to an ought. Since one must never do injustice, one must never return injustice for injustice, because to return injustice for injustice is to do injustice. Put as a piece of elementary moral mathematics, two wrongs don't make a right. But if one must never return injustice for injustice, one must never work injury or do evil to anyone in return for having suffered it, since there is no difference between doing evil to men and doing injustice. The proposition that one must not return evil for evil is presented, in the most emphatic terms, as a paradox which the Many will never accept (49c). One may well ask where the paradox lies.

It is easy to read the proposition that one ought never do injustice or wrong as tautological: one ought not do what one ought to do. But Socrates has already argued that to do injustice is to corrupt the soul, and that life is not worth living when the soul is corrupted; if that is so, it is unreasonable to avoid death at the cost of injustice.[15] But no issues except issues of logic are relevant to the truth of a tautology. Manifestly, much must depend on the content of the concept of justice.

Part of that content is indicated by the equivalence between doing injustice and working injury or doing evil to men. But this raises a further question: for the equivalence, on its face, seems either to confirm tautology or to involve fallacy.

The notion of injury has eroded in English to the point where it is often used very nearly as a synonym for damage or harm, while yet retaining, as often happens, the overtones of a former force. Falling down stairs injures a man when it harms him; but it is an injury to push him even if no harm results. In the same way, defamation may be an injury even when it causes no harm. On the other hand, if you drop your watch and break it, or your barn is struck by lightning and partly burnt, your watch and your barn have been damaged, but it is hardly apt to say that they have been injured. In general, one can do damage to a man and so harm him, and that harm will be injury. But one can injure a man without harming him, and damage an inanimate object but not injure it.

What is back of all this, of course, is etymology. Harm is Old English, and implies evil done or suffered. Damage derives through Norman French from Latin *damnum*, meaning any sort of hurt, harm, or loss. Injury, on the other hand, derives from *injuria*, which in turn derives from *in jus*, contrary to law or right. Thus at common law, certain harms are dismissed as *damna sine injuria*, losses which the law will refuse to shift and rather let lie where they fall.

Wrongful injury is etymological tautology but good modern speech, and the ambiguity in injury between harm and wrongful harm matches the ambiguity of Socrates' expressions *kakourgein* and *kakōs poiein*, to work evil or do ill, with precision. Does Socrates mean that you ought not return injury with a *wrong*? Or does he mean that you ought not return injury with a *harm*? There is a considerable difference. If he means the first, the argument is, as he presents it to be, merely an amplification of the premise that one ought never do injustice. If he means the second, his argument has led to a conclusion equivalent to the teachings of Jesus of Nazareth.[16]

It seems clear that Socrates cannot be understood to mean that it is wrong to harm anyone if harm is understood in a physical sense. For in the first place, he fought with bravery and great distinction at Potidaea, Amphipolis, and Delium (see *Symposium* 220d-221b, *Laches* 181b), and he mentions his work as a soldier in the *Apology* (28e), not as a fault, but as an example of devotion to duty. But it would be odd to think you can run a sword through someone without physically harming him. Again, he agrees with Polus in the *Gorgias* that it is sometimes just to put men to death, to exile them, or to confiscate their property (470b-c), and the *Crito*, though it denies that Socrates was rightly condemned, in that he was not guilty of the charges brought against him, does not deny that the Laws may rightfully exact execution. One might sum up the situation by saying that execution is no *injuria*, but *damnum* aplenty. It would seem, then, that the conclusion that one ought never return injury for injury is a direct implication of the claim that one ought never do injustice or return injustice for injustice—which is, of course, exactly as Socrates presents it.

"See to it, Crito, that you do not agree against your real opinion, for I know that few men think or will ever think it true" (49d). The reader may be pardoned for inquiring where the paradox in rejecting wrongful injury lies. The answer is in important part that it lies in rejecting the rightfulness of retribution, the returning of harm for wrong.

The retributionist, of course, would claim as heartily as Socrates himself that one ought never do wrong, and therefore that one ought not return wrong for wrong. He would argue, however, that when wrong has in fact been done, there is duty (this is the strong form of the theory) or a right (the weaker form) to inflict harm on the wrong-doer. Because that infliction is either a duty or a right, it does not involve returning wrong for wrong; on the contrary, it involves (strong theory) returning right for wrong, or (weak theory) returning what is not wrong for wrong. It will be observed that on the strong form of the theory, to abstain from retribution is to abstain from a duty, and is itself morally wrong. The weaker version does not thus make mercy immoral.

Both Socrates and the retributionist, then, accept the proposition that one ought never do injustice—or at least the form of words. The difference between them lies in their conception of justice.

For the retributive theory, justice is connected with debt; it is no accident that 'ought' is in origin a past tense of 'owe', nor that 'duty' derives through Norman French from *debere*. The verb *tribuo* means to assign, apportion, allot; *retribuo*, to return or repay; *retributio*, a recompense or repayment, specifically of desert whether good or ill. The retributionist believes that justice is relational as debt is relational. There is some evidence, indeed, that this may put the cart before the horse: from the fragmentary evidence of the earliest remains of Roman law, the Law of the Twelve Tables, it appears that debt may be been relational as justice is relational.[17] This much, at least, is clear: if I borrow, I owe. For the retributionist, if I wrong, I also owe. The debt incurred by wrongful injury must be discharged by returning harm to the wrongdoer, if it is to be discharged at all.

The debt analogy introduces a second main theme of retribution, that of proportionality: proper payment is reckoned in terms of the amount of debt incurred. It is often said that retribution is simply revenge. This is false, for the reason, among others, that retribution functions not only as a measure of vengeance but a limitation on vengeance. It is right, not wrong, which is to be returned for wrong, and as early as the Code of Hammurabi it is insisted, "Thus much shalt thou take, *and no more*."[18] Proportionality coupled with the strong form of retribution produces the Talian Law. Under settled and civilized conditions of life, it will seem savage that eye should go for eye, tooth for tooth, life for life; but there are conditions under which the Talian Law is a law of mercy, placing limits on the imagination in an area where humankind has often proved overly ingenious.

Retribution is commonly associated, in its Talian form, with the Pentateuch: "Behold, I set before you this day a blessing and a curse."[19] But it was quite as deeply rooted in ancient Greek as in ancient Jewish thought, and produced much that is distinctive in Greek cosmology and Greek drama. The earliest surviving fragment of Greek philosophy is a text of Anaximander, perserved by Simplicius:

The source of coming-to-be for existing things is that into which destruction too, happens, "according to necessity; for they pay penalty and retribution to each other for their injustice according to the assessment of time," as he describes it in these rather poetical terms.[20]

The legal order has been projected on to the universe at large. "They" are the warring opposites, hot and cold, wet and dry, light and dark, which commit injustice upon each other as they alternately triumph in the cycle of days and seasons, alternately take as their province more than a just or equal share. Time, acting as judge, corrects the balance. This theme, in altered form, persists in Heraclitus, and is linked to that psychology of the tragic passions, the cycle of *Hybris* and *Nemesis*, by which Herodotus and Thucydides interpret human history, and Aeschylus and Sophocles human life. The theme of retribution, in Greek hands, was one of immense conceptual and artistic fertility.

The account Socrates offers in the *Crito* contradicts the rightfulness of retribution, not by refuting it, but by making the constellation of concepts on which it depends irrelevant to the moral issue with which it is meant to deal. Retribution is backward-looking: the justice of inflicting present harm is conditioned by the fact and extent of past wrongdoing. But if justice has to do with the good of the soul, then the criterion for determining whether action is right or wrong is benefit or harm to the soul, and the existence of past wrong done or suffered is irrelevant to this except as it conditons the present state of the soul.

The aim of just punishment is to make bad men better, to increase the measure of their human excellence, and thereby the measure of their happiness or well-being (see *Gorgias* 476b-477a, 478d-e). Therefore, as it is better to suffer injustice than to do it, so it is also true that the unjust man, if he knew what is in his own interest, as he does not, would seek punishment for himself because of its medicinal value, for its effect of purifying the soul from the disease of wickedness. Punishment is imposed, when it is imposed rightly, not simply because of past wrongdoing, but for the sake of the soul of the wrongdoer—or if he is beyond cure, for the sake of himself and his fellows.[21] This theory is distinct from the retributive theory in that it does not place positive as distinct from instrumental value on human suffering as such, and does not measure the wickedness of an agent by the wickedness of his act.

But it is not the humanitarian doctrine that some critics have seen in it.[22] In the first place, it countenances simple extermination in the case of incurables (*Gorgias* 512a). In the second place, although it attaches only instrumental value to the infliction of suffering, it treats suffering itself as an intrinsic means of cure. Aristotle later put the point succinctly:

If the virtues are concerned with actions and passions, and every action and every passion is accompanied by pleasure and pain, for this reason also virtue will be concerned with pleasure and pain. This is indicated also by the fact that punishment is inflicted by these means; for it is a kind of cure, and it is the nature of cures to be effected by contraries.[23]

The use of the medical analogy should not obscure a fundamental distinction: the proposition that punishment should aim at the good of the soul, the human excellence of the person punished, is logically independent of the proposition that this aim is best effected by the infliction of pain. No doubt it is true, as Aeschylus said, that it is possible to learn by suffering, πάθῳ μαθεῖν; but it is also true, as Plato observed in the *Timaeus* (86e), that, "Where pains are concerned, the soul derives much badness from the body."

The Socratic concern for the good of the soul has often been misunderstood to be a form of ethical, or even psychological, egoism. That view confuses the goodness of satisfying a desire with the goodness of what is desired. The truth is that one condition of human excellence is concern for the human excellence of others, a point made with precision in the *Republic*. Polemarchus has quoted Simonides' dictum that it is just to render every man his due—a dictum which, restated in Justinian's *Institutes*,[24] was to play an important role in later discussions of 'natural law'. When Socrates points out the lack of usefulness of the slogan—what is it, after all, that is 'due', and to whom—Polemarchus undertakes to make the dictum more precise by defining what is due in terms of helping friends and harming enemies. Socrates rejects this on the ground that it can no more be the function of goodness to do harm than of heat to cool or of drought to produce moisture: it is never right to harm anyone (*Republic* I 335a-e, cf. *Apology* 25c-e, 41d). Justice, and virtue in general, is analogous to an art, which aims at some good for its object. Socrates will later conclude that, "Any kind of authority, in the state or in private life, must, in its character of authority, consider solely what is best for those under its care" (*Republic* I 345d-e). It cannot be a function of justice to diminish excellence in others. Even in dealing with bad men, it cannot be just to make bad men worse.

On Socratic principles, then, there is no ambiguity between harm and wrongful harm, for to harm a man is to make him worse as a man, to diminish his human excellence. Retribution is injustice. The apparently tautological principle that one ought never do injustice is equivalent to the principle that one ought never so act as to diminish human excellence in oneself or in another—and that is not tautology, but honest paradox. It stands in direct contravention to the moral standards of fifth-century Athens, accurately represented by Polemarchus, in which injury to enemies was confirmation of one's own excellence. And though it sits lightly on the lips today—one gets used to hearing these things—it takes but scant experience of men and events to realize that, as a practical matter, the principle remains no less paradoxical than when Socrates first uttered it.

To injure or harm something, to corrupt it, is to make it worse with respect to its own proper excellence. Harm, of course, involves bodily harm: but there is an issue of priority, for soul is more valuable than body (48a). The *Crito* assumes (49d) and the *Gorgias* maintains (474b ff. and passim) that it is better to suffer injustice than to do it, because doing injustice must inevitably harm the soul, while suffering it need harm no more than the body. In a similar way, it may be just to put men to death, if their souls are corrupted beyond cure (*Gorgias* 512a, 525a-c), or run the risk of wounds and death in battle, or inflict them, when Laws and the City require—or in a different sort of battle, at another soldiers' station, to suffer execution by reason of an unjust verdict, if the alternative is to do injustice to the Laws.

The Speech of the Laws of Athens (50a-54d)

The question whether Socrates should escape has been reduced to the question whether, if he escapes, he will injure those whom he least ought, and whether he will break agreements it is just to keep. These questions are now answered in a dialogue within the dialogue, between Socrates and the Laws of Athens.

Plato's personification of the Laws may strike the modern reader as a mere literary device. But the Laws function very like the chorus in a Greek tragedy: they participate in the action, and do not merely observe it, but they also judge it from a perspective which lies outside it. The *Crito*'s personification of law was much admired in antiquity—Cicero, for example, following Demosthenes, imitated it in the *First Catalinarian*—and was more than a literary device, since the ancients tended independently to conceive of the laws and the commonwealth as a juridical person.[25] In the *Crito*, the personification of law answers to an assumption in legal ontology. Statements about a legal order cannot be analyzed without remainder into sets of statements about individual human beings, any more than statements about that creature of law, the corporation, can be analyzed without remainder into sets of statements about its members. An indication of this is that a legal order may be said to exist, or not to exist, or to have ceased to exist, and this is not equivalent to any set of statements about individuals living, dead, or yet unborn. As a connected point, it may be observed that there are duties owed to the legal order, and that it may owe duties in return. The personification of the Laws of Athens answers to a fact—however it is to be analyzed—of legal ontology. The laws and constitution of Athens exist, and their existence is a function of their authority, for breach of their authority tends to their destruction.

The speech of the Laws is rhetoric, rhetoric of such force that when they are done, Socrates turns and says, "Crito, my dear and faithful friend, I think I hear these things as the Corybants think they hear the pipes, and the droning murmur of their words sounds within me and makes me incapable of hearing aught else." And Crito too is silenced. The style of the speech combines familiar intimacy, and indeed tenderness toward Socrates, with a majestic and authoritative solemnity. This combination of incompatibles is a conjuror's trick, which only a master of prose style could play.

Because the speech of the Laws is rhetoric, it has been discounted as argument. But it is in this speech that the reasoning of the *Crito* is brought to conclusion, and the speech therefore cannot be dismissed. It lacks the superb irony of the speech of defense in the *Apology*, and is more overtly dialectical in its argument. But it too is philosophical rhetoric, aimed at persuasion based on truth and indifferent to gratification, not at flattery based on gratification and indifferent to truth. The Laws in the *Crito* speak as physicians of soul. Their speech is not "at random": it is a unified and organic whole, with head, trunk, and limbs, organized around a single self-consistent principle, the primacy of justice. Their speech appeals, as rhetoric should, to powerful emotions: to religious feelings, to love of country, to gratitude for the gift of life and education, to the moral sentiments which attach to promise-keeping. The speech also meets, point by point, the prudential considerations Crito urged in favor of escape. But though the speech appeals to emotion, it does not rest on emotional appeal; though it deals with prudential considerations, it does not turn on them. It is both rhetoric and dialectic—dialectical rhetoric—even though it is only intermittently cast in dialogue form. Socrates had earlier said that he would be persuaded only by the *logos* which on reflection proved best to him. The speech of the Laws presents that *logos* at its very head: escape is unjust because it involves the doing of injury. The *logos* rests on two premises which Socrates and Crito, in conversation, have already agreed to, and the Laws, as they continue, elicit by questioning further agreement at every major step of the way.

Partly because the speech of the Laws is rhetorical, and partly because of the close relation between the *Crito* and the *Apology*, the *Crito* has been understood as a merely biographical document. M. Croiset remarked, "It is a misunderstanding to see in it a kind of abstract thesis about the respect owed to law by the citizen,"[26] and proceeded to read the dialogue as an exhibition of Socrates' beauty of character and concern for consistency with the affirmation of his past life. More recent critics have seen in the *Crito* a portrait of Socrates as Existential Hero, man in his loneliness affirming his fateful freedom, and thereby his existence, possessed of absolute liberty of choice in the face of death. The *Crito* itself tells a different story. Socrates goes to his death on the basis of a *logos*, an account or argument—a kind of 'commitment', no doubt, but a commitment to thinking things through. Many of the arguments on which the discussion turns are represented as having been discussed and agreed upon before; but they are raised in order to be reexamined and reaffirmed, and the warrant for their acceptance lies, not in past agreement, but in their truth. The claim is not that Socrates should stand by past agreements out of consistency with past life, but that those agreements, recognized once as true, remain true still. Socrates went to his death on the basis of an argument. No less than Parmenides had done in metaphysics, he expects us to judge by reason his strife-contested proof. He chose to die rather than escape because he was convinced by reasoning that it was right to die and wrong to escape; and that reasoning is brought to conclusion in the speech of the Laws of Athens. Any account of the *Crito* which stresses the beauty of the man to the neglect of his argument may justly be suspected of missing the beauty of the man.

The Laws of Athens begin their speech (50a-b) with an astonishing charge: that Socrates, if he attempts to escape, will thereby attempt so far as in him lies to destroy the Laws and the City. The reason given is that no city can exist and not be overturned in which judgments judicially rendered are without authority (50b). Granting that this is so, the Laws infer that Socrates' escape will constitute a harm to the City. If it cannot be a work of justice to do injustice, of excellence to

diminish excellence in another, of goodness to do harm, this is ground
for supposing that escape is unjust.

The principle that judgments judicially rendered are authorative is
itself described as law (50b), and it is precisely this law which Socrates will break if he escapes. That law, or principle is one which is
fundamental to the existence of a legal system, in which courts have
a central role in the application of law. The application of law requires
application through lawful agency, and it is the foundation of a legal
system that judgments judicially rendered, unless set aside by legal
means, are authoritative.[27]

This hardly suffices to explain, however, the truly extraordinary
proposition that an attempt by Socrates to escape implies an attempt,
so far as in him lies, to destroy the City and its laws. The City of
Athens will not be physically destroyed by the escape of one prisoner;
breaking jail is not like sacking Troy. Nor will the escape of one prisoner overthrow the government; breaking jail is not like causing a
revolution.

Destruction aside, where is there harm? In plain utilitarian terms,
Socrates' escape would probably have benefited Athens: it would
have relieved the City of the odium attaching to the unjust conviction of a distinguished and widely honored man (cf. *Apology* 38c).
Passing from City to citizens, Socrates' escape would have salved the
consciences of many of his jurors, and of other citizens, too; a number of the dicasts who voted to condemn him must surely have done
so with reluctance, and because he refused to suggest exile as a counterpenalty at the trial; they had since had time for second thoughts
(cf. *Apology* 37a-c). Then there is the grief of Socrates' family and
friends to consider, and finally there is Socrates himself; for though
he was willing to think of death as a good, he knew as well as any
man that it is also the irrevocable loss of all that one loves in life. As
he remarks in the *Apology* (34d), he is not "of oak and rock," but
born of man (cf. *Phaedo* 98e-99a).[28]

There are, in short, multiple utilitarian grounds for supposing that
Socrates should escape, and no ordinary grounds for claiming that
escape would harm the City or its laws. Why then is that proposition
to be maintained?

The key lies in the nature of judicial authority. To escape is to
deny, not by word but by deed, not by uttering negative statements
but by positive breach, the authority of the verdict and sentence. That
sentence was rendered according to law and, *as legal*, owes its authority precisely to that source. To deny the authority of a given sentence

so rendered is to deny authority to any sentence so rendered; but this is to deny authority to law itself, since it is to deny authority to its application. Since the application of law is essential to the existence of law, to act in breach of a given application is—by so much—destructive of all law. Since law without application is not law, and a city without law is not a city, the Laws of Athens claim that Socrates, if he escapes, will attempt so far as in him lies to destroy the City and its laws. Aristotle remarks, presumably with the *Crito* in mind, "Judicial decisions are useless if they take no effect; and if society cannot exist without them, neither can it exist without the execution of them."[29] This account of judicial authority rests, then, on a universalization argument, found nowhere else in ancient philosophy. It explains why, if *this* judgment as judicially rendered is not authoritative, then *no* judgment as judicially rendered is authoritative. This principle, it is claimed, is fundamental to the existence of a legal system.

The argument of the Laws is not primarily contractual, but delictual: its gist lies not in breach of agreement, but in claim of injury. The brunt of the charge against Socrates is not that, if he escapes, he will break a promise, but that he will to the degree that he is able destroy the laws and the City. The charge matches with precision the structure of the premises which Socrates and Crito have already accepted.

The universalization principle attaches to the existence of a legal order. It is not, *per se*, a moral principle, as is shown by the fact that it may be consistently accepted by an anarchist, who believes that law is an evil and should be destroyed. So the universalization argument of the *Crito* must be sharply distinguished from the moral universalization argument offered by Kant in formulating the categorical imperative. Nowhere in ancient moral theory is it suggested that the test of wrongful action is that the maxim of the action cannot be universalized without contradiction, perhaps for the reason that that test, if it is not purely formal and empty, is incoherent.[30] Breach of the authority of law does not, in the *Crito*, imply immorality without the additional premises, not supplied by any sort of universalization argument, that it is wrong to do injury or return it, and right to abide by agreements when it is just to do so. Universalization is not offered as an independent test of right and wrong, but as a principle attaching to legal validity. Breach of *this* verdict is destructive of *all* law precisely because this verdict issued from a source legally empowered to render it. That source, in the constitution of Athens under the restored democracy, was ultimately the Assembly, and derivatively, in the case of Socrates, the court which tried him.

It is important to see that the argument of the Laws involves a trick of perspective. On the one hand, the Laws are parties to the argument, and as such, claim all to be equally authoritative: obey, or convince us to the contrary. The conceptual foundation for this claim is that they are all equally supported by the universalization principle which attaches to legal validity. But the Laws are not merely a set of rules: they are an ordered set, forming a legal system, and that legal system exists. Their argument shows that some laws are more fundamental than others; specifically, the law which Socrates will break if he escapes, that judgments judicially rendered are authoritative, is fundamental to the existence of a legal system, a thing which is not true, say, of a rule dealing with the wearing of red hats during the month of Thargelion. Viewed in this way, the argument of the Laws still rests on a universalization principle, but in respect of application: the difference between a dead legal system and a live one is that a live system is applied; dead law consists only in rules with application.

The Laws of Athens, as characters in the dialogue, demand obedience to all laws. In this they are faithful to their character as laws, which do not offer themselves to the citizen as mere recommendations among which he may pick or choose, but as obligations. But the foundation of the argument goes to the issue of existence, and viewed in this light, their argument does not prove that every breach of a given law is destructive of the legal order, that it is a primary duty to obey all laws taken distributively. It shows rather that there is a duty *either* to obey all laws, *or* to accept the legal consequences of disobedience when imposed by a court, and even, as in Socrates' case, to accept those consequences when there has in fact been no disobedience. The fundamental duty imposed by the legal order is not blind obedience to each of its rules—some of which, after all, may be unjust—but of fidelity to the legal order itself.

A legal system defines the conditions of validity under which given rules are authoritative. Put briefly, authority implies validity. But there is more to authority than validity. There is also the issue of scope. A Thessalian there domiciled who refused to obey an Athenian law respecting the wearing of red hats during the month of Thargelion could hardly be said to harm Athens by denying the authority of its laws—though he would deny that authority, and rightly, so far as it concerned himself. Thus, though breach implies denial, denial does not imply breach. The authority of law involves scope. How is this to be explained?

Not, certainly, in terms of geography. No doubt every municipal legal system is the order of some territory, but territory can scarcely define the scope of its obligation. Citizenship may bind beyond borders, and different laws may govern the citizens of different jurisdictions within the same borders. The Laws of Athens put scope and breach on a different basis. There is an agreement between Socrates and the Laws, and it is a term of that agreement that Socrates is to abide by such judgments as the City may render (50c). Legal authority does not, so to speak, exist 'in air': it is relational, and one basis of that relation is agreement. A Thessalonian may deny the authority of Athenian law because he has entered no agreement to obey it. Socrates, however, has entered an agreement with the Laws of Athens to live as a citizen. He therefore stands within the scope of authority of Athenian law, and his escape will constitute a harm to Athens, as breach of that authority.

All of this, of course, depends upon the existence of agreement, and in arguing that point the Laws of Athens probably present the best evidence that now remains extant of Greek analysis of the law of contracts. The Laws, certainly, speak very like lawyers. M. Beauchet remarks:

It is difficult to know whether the Greek jurisconsults succeeded in distinguishing the notion of the 'cause' of obligations as precisely as modern authors have done, or even whether they understood the idea of 'cause' as the Roman jurisconsults did. Nevertheless, it is certain that Attic jurisprudence arrived at very nearly the same results as Roman law in the different cases of obligations without cause, and on illicit cause. It may be that cause was not considered in Athens, any more than in Rome, as an essential condition for the validity of contracts. But in every case, its absence, or its illicit character, permits one who is under obligation without cause or on illicit cause to withdraw from his obligation and to claim that the contract is void.[31]

Pacta sunt servanda, no doubt. But no legal system treats all agreements as creating a binding obligation. The tool for distinguishing enforceable agreements from those which are not is, at common law, consideration, and in civil law, cause. "By the cause of an obligation, one must understand the immediate aim which the party who obligates himself intends to obtain by obligating himself."[32] Cause implies an intent to enter legal relations, and the immediate aim of an obligation may be defined in terms of a recognized legal category—for example, debt. Cause is illicit if the immediate aim is contrary to law or right; an obligation is without cause if it is gratuitous, that is, if nothing is obtained by it. The Laws of Athens begin by showing, in effect, that Socrates' agreement to live as a citizen is binding by reason of cause which is not illicit.

Does Socrates have some charges to lay against the Laws, that he should undertake to destroy them? It was through them that his father and mother were able to enter wedlock and legitimately beget him, and through them too that his father was required to educate him in a way befitting an Athenian. Can Socrates find fault with those laws (50d-e)? He agrees that he cannot, and the Laws therefore claim to be elder and more august parents than those from whose flesh he sprang: Socrates, as did his fathers before him, owes his birth and education, his very existence as a civilized human being, to the Laws.

This is a claim of debt, a claim that there is cause at the foundation of Socrates' agreement, and that it is not illicit. In virtue of this claim, the Laws hold that Socrates is their slave (50e). If slavery is a status in which a person is subject to penal liability without legal rights,[33] or (a weaker sense) a status in which a person may be a chattel, owned by another, then Socrates is in neither sense a slave. He is owned by no man, and has many legal rights: he is—or was until his condemnation—a free man *under* law. But that is just the point. The claim of slavery is a claim of authority, which the Laws explicate by an analogy extended from paternal authority under Athenian law. That authority was less extreme than the Roman *patria potestas*, with its *jus vitae ac necris*, power of life and death, but it was strong enough even in Plato's time to allow power to expose newborn children, mastership of daughters until given in marriage, and power to disown grown sons, depriving them of rights of family worship, their patrimony, and perhaps even their name.[34] Paternal authority in Athens was no light thing: within a limited sphere, it did what even a court could not do. But that authority was exercised, like that of a court, under law, and specifically under those laws governing marriage and the rearing of children.

The Laws, therefore, in claiming authority superior to that of Socrates' own parents, are stating a fact, since paternal authority is derived from law. Furthermore, their inference from that fact is accurate. Where a relation of authority exists, whether that of a father or a master or that of the law itself, those over whom authority is exercised do not have a right to do as they are done by. Authority confers rights and imposes duties asymmetrically, or as the Laws put it, unevenly or unequally (50e-51a). If A has authority over B, then A has rights in respect of B which B does not have in respect of A. This is specifically true of the authority of courts in respect of punishment. Thus, even if it were true that Socrates has been wronged at the hands of the Laws by the imposition of an unjust sentence, it would not in the least follow that he thereby has a right by escaping to return evil to those who may rightfully punish him, any more than he has a right to evade the duties of military service, and its attendant dangers.

The claim of slavery, combined as it is with the claim of debt, has religious overtones as well. In the *Phaedo* (62b-c), Socrates holds that he and all mankind are possessions of the gods, good masters whom men are bound to obey and serve. The Laws of Athens assume that the gift of life and education is a gift which imposes religious duties: that obedience to law and country is a matter, not only of justice, but of holiness and reverence and divine apportionment. As it is impious to injure the parents who gave one life, so it is still more impious to injure the Laws through whom life was given. Greek religion was rooted in the family cultus, but still more in the City and its festivals,[35] and the association of law and religion ran deep in the Athenian polity. That is why Socrates could be subjected to public prosecution for impiety, and brought before the King Archon, who was both king and priest.[36] In the last of Plato's works, the *Laws* (VI 762e; cf. III 700a, IX 715d), the Athenian Stranger holds that service to the laws is service to the gods.

The Laws of Athens, then, base their claim of slavery on a characteristic ancient attitude toward the life of the individual in relation to his city. Aristotle, many years after the *Crito* was written, spoke for traditional Greek feeling when he said:

The state [*polis*] is by nature clearly prior to the family and to the individual, since the whole is of necessity prior to the part; for example, if the whole body is destroyed, there will be no foot or hand. . . . The proof that the state is a creation of nature and is prior to the individual is that the individual, when isolated, is not self-sufficing; and therefore he is like a part in relation to the whole. But he who is unable to live in society, or has no need because he is sufficient for himself, must be either a beast or a god; he is no part of a state.[37]

This expresses with some precision the basis of the account the Laws here offer: it emphasizes the dependence of the individual on the social order, a dependence which is the foundation of allegiance, and thereby of the duty of fidelity to law. This, of course, is a very different thing from the nineteenth- and twentieth-century political perversion that the whole duty of man is exhausted in his relation to the state, a claim which neither Aristotle, Plato, nor Socrates accepted. In matters of justice, states, like individuals, may err. The Biblical injunction that thou shalt not follow a multitude to do evil is one which Socrates would most emphatically have accepted (see 48a), and it is deprived of meaning if what the multitude do, when organized, is by definition good.

The effect of this is to give force to Socrates' earlier question to Crito: "If we escape from here without persuading the City, will we not do evil to someone, and someone whom we *least* ought?" (49e). The Laws have shown that they are among those whom Socrates ought least to injure. To do harm to them is more than to do harm: it is to do impious wrong. That wrong is so much the worse for the fact that the Laws not only gave Socrates birth and education, but also, instead of issuing a rude command, gave him opportunity to persuade them to the contrary if they were doing something wrong.[38] Once again, the argument goes not only to the existence of cause, but to its licitness. As an axiom of jurisprudence, laws which admit of persuasion to what is right are laws based, however imperfectly, on reason rather than fiat.

The Laws next turn to argue their case for the existence of an agreement between themselves and Socrates. They hold that to live as a citizen of Athens implies an undertaking to live according to the laws of that city, acknowledging their authority, and specifically the authority of judgments judicially rendered. "To whom would a city be pleasing without laws?" (53a). This agreement is not expressed but implied, resting not on words but on action and the conduct of a life. In one sense, Socrates was born a citizen of Athens, or to be quite precise, acquired rights under Athenian law when he was accepted into his father's house at the *Amphidromia*, five days after birth. But he did not come of age until seventeen, or perhaps eighteen, and until that time he was an infant, in the unetymological sense of one who has not reached his majority. To borrow an Aristotelian distinction, his citizenship was neither voluntary nor involuntary, but nonvoluntary; he was legally incapable of decision in the matter, which rested with his father. But upon being admitted to the rights of manhood (cf. 52d), he gained power to choose whether to maintain citizenship or abandon it. He chose to maintain it—and thus voluntarily entered an agreement which he maintained throughout his life.

It is of the essence of agreement that it be voluntary, and if it is not voluntary, it is invalid.[39] The Laws of Athens maintain that Socrates' agreement to live as a citizen was voluntary on the simple ground that he had a choice in the matter: he could have gone elsewhere, either to an Athenian colony or a foreign city (51d). His consent to live as a citizen was not obtained by coercion, or by misrepresentation or mistake, or—this last perhaps a testimony to the awesome power of Greek high-pressure salesmanship—through too little time to decide, a species of undue influence (52e). He had seventy years to decide;[40] there had not been too little time. He has had ample opportunity to inform himself of the workings of the City and its laws, and how judicial decisions are rendered; there has been no misrepresentation, nor are there grounds for a plea of mistake. He has since the time he was admitted to the rights of manhood been at liberty to leave Athens for another country, taking with him what is his;[41] there has been no coercion. On the contrary, there is every indication—defenses apart—that Socrates' agreement to live as a citizen was not only voluntary, but enthusiastic. The City and its laws must have surpassingly pleased him, since he founded a family in it, and journied abroad less often than the halt, the lame, and the blind (53a). So Socrates is bound by the agreement his citizenship implies; because of that agreement, he stands within the scope of authority of Athenian law; because he stands within that scope, escape will imply breach and wrongful harm to the legal order.

The Laws, then, propound a contractual theory of citizenship—but it is well to avoid confusion in so speaking. The claim that Socrates has agreed with the Laws to live as a citizen means, and means only, that he has voluntarily accepted a given legal status, distinguished in Athenian law from the status of a metic, a freedman, or a slave. That status confers legal rights and imposes legal duties; one of those duties is to abide by the decisions of courts; therefore, acceptance of the status of citizenship involves an implied agreement so to abide. There is nothing in this of the "Social Contract" as that term was understood by Plato, or as we understand it from Hobbes. The outlines of the Social Contract theory of the state are presented, more ably than its own proponents might have done, at the beginning of book II of the *Republic*. The theory is a developed version of the beliefs of Callicles and Thrasymachus, and it is a theory of justice. It rests on egoism as a fundamental premise, and derives legal positivism as a conclusion. It is held to represent the teachings of common sense—what the Many believe.

What the Many believe is that law and justice are good, if good at all, in the same way that work and medical treatment are good. Glaucon begins his account of the Social Contract by distinguishing three kinds of goods. Some things are good in that we welcome them for their own sake; for example, harmless pleasures which have no further consequences. Some things are good in that we delight in them both for their own sake and for their consequences; for example, thinking and sight and health. And some things are good, not because they are accepted for their own sake, but solely for the sake of their consequences, since they are burdensome and painful but beneficial; for example, gymnastic exercise, moneymaking, and medical treatment. Socrates claims that justice is the second kind of good—we may recall the analogy between justice and health—whereas most people think that justice, if it is good at all, is of the third sort—to be pursued for its consequences, but in itself an affliction (*Republic* II 357b-358c). The reason is that people practice justice not because they want to, but because they must. The Many believe that men 'by nature' seek their own preservation and the satisfaction of their own individual desires and needs, and this at the expense and to the injury of their fellows. Put in ordinary terms, this is a way of saying that it is by nature better to do injustice than to suffer it, and Glaucon, speaking for the Many, so states the case. It is, of course, an exact reversal of the Socratic claim that it is better to suffer injustice than to do it. Those who do not have the power to get the benefit of injustice while escaping the harm of doing it band together and make laws and compacts with each other, and call right and just whatever the law prescribes. So justice is a middle way between the best thing, which is to do injustice with impunity, and the worst, which is to suffer it without power to retaliate. So justice is not good for its own sake; it is onerous, and accepted only for its consequences, and for lack of power to do wrong without suffering it. Every man by nature pursues his own advantage, but "by violence of law" is led to honor equality. Just and unjust men alike, if given the ring of Gyges, so that they might be invisible, would behave in exactly the same way: unjustly. No one is just voluntarily, but only under constraint.

This is, of course, a theory of natural law, for the expression 'by nature', in Greek as in English, wavers between the descriptive and the normative: it is used not only to describe how men in fact behave, but to justify their behaving that way—compare much recent rubbish about 'ethology' and 'territorial imperatives', or the Athenian emissaries in the Melian Dialogue. The social contract theory which Glaucon expounds in the *Republic* rests on the doctrine of Callicles in the *Gorgias* (483a-b) that by nature it is worse to suffer evil than to do it, while by law (or convention) it is worse to do it than to suffer it; law is based on a social contract which allows the many weak to protect themselves against the few strong. In the same vein, the sophist Antiphon in a fragment of his lost work *On Truth* recovered at Oxyrhynchus claims that "most things legally just are inimical to nature,"[42] and Hippias of Elis, speaking in Plato's *Protagoras* (337c-d), calls law a despot because it constrains men against nature.

Callicles, of course, anticipates Nietzsche: the moral judgments men form according to their laws constitute a slave morality which the strong man, like a lion, will trample under foot, imposing his will according to his strength. Both Nietzsche and Callicles proclaim their doctrine as revolutionary, a 'transvaluation of all values', in Nietzsche's phrase; but the truth is they were revolutionaries without a cause. Callicles is not merely saying what many men believe but are ashamed to say (*Gorgias* 492d), but as Socrates shows, speaking in defense of the slave morality he condemns and in his heart accepts as deeply as any of his fellows; for if natural justice is a function of power, then slave morality, so long as the slaves have power to enforce it, is natural justice. Thus, by a ready interchange, the ideal of the *Übermensch* becomes the ideal of the *Volk*, and a doctrine proclaimed as revolutionary becomes allied to worship of what is—whatever it is. It has remained for modern commentators to find in this a celebration of the liberal temper in Greek politics, and the joys of the open society. Callicles' image of the strong man as lion is most apt: the lion is handsome at a distance, and dangerous even if you have weapons which only intelligence can forge; but on nearer acquaintance, he proves to be an animal of vulgar appetites and gross habit. Like a dead mackerel in the moonlight, he shines, but he stinks.

The Social Contract theory of government rests law on the will of the parties, on an agreement between man and man. But the agreement contemplated in the *Crito* is not between man and man, but between man and the law itself. It consists in voluntary acceptance of the status of citizenship, a status which implies an agreement to abide by the decisions of courts. It implies nothing about the origins—moral, analytic, or historical—of law.

Though the voluntary assumption of the status of citizenship may be called contractural, as resting on agreement, it is not in any legal sense a contract. A contract, Athenian or modern, creates rights and duties *in personam*, affecting the legal relations of the parties only as parties to the contract, not their legal relations to the world at large. Furthermore, within limits prescribed by law and morality, the terms of agreement in contract are open, left to the will of the parties. A legal status, by contrast—and citizenship in Athenian law was a palmary example of this—is closed, in that the law itself defines the rights and duties which attach to it; furthermore, it affects not merely one legal relationship, but rights and duties at large. It is further worth remarking that if voluntary acceptance of the status of citizenship is not a contract *at* law, neither is it a contract *with* law; for in contract, the law binds the parties, whereas the middle term in this agreement is not legal but moral, since the law itself is a party to it.

Granting the existence of an implied agreement to abide by the decisions of courts, the fact remains that Socrates has been unjustly condemned. Why, after all, should an unjust conviction not be sufficient warrant for escape?

One might argue that this too is an implication of the agreement to live as a citizen. Laws, to be laws, must be applied. To be applied, they must be applied by men, who are always fallible and often prejudiced. To accept citizenship, to enter an implied agreement to abide by the decisions of courts, is to accept the fact that law will sometimes be wrongfully applied, that given decisions may be marked by the specific kind of injustice which issues from falseness to fact or mistake in its classification. Because this is so, wrongful conviction provides no ground for claiming a right to escape.

Still, what is at issue is an unjust sentence of death. Even Hobbes, who held that men on entering civil society transfer all natural rights to Leviathan, yet reserved one: the natural right of the citizen, innocent or guilty, to escape punishment, and especially death, if he could, on the ground that no man can be obligated to accept a consequence of contract inconsistent with the cause for which he entered it.[43] The *Crito* does not assume a theory of natural rights. But given that one ought to abide by agreements when it is just to do so, it is hardly clear that one ought to abide by agreements when so to abide requires the suffering of injustice.

But in fact, the premise of agreement does not stand as an independent reason for refusing to escape. It serves rather to show that Socrates stands within the scope of legal authority, and that therefore his refusal to abide by the decision of the court will constitute an injury to law. The primary charge the Laws lay against him is that escape implies an attempt, so far as in him lies, to encompass the destruction of the City.

The Laws next turn (53a-54a) to the practical or prudential question of whether escape would in fact be preferable to death. In the *Apology* (37d-e), Socrates refused to propose exile as a counterpenalty to death, for the reason, among others, that if his fellow citizens cannot bear his peculiar inquiries, it is unreasonable to think that others will. The Laws now repeat this argument, with greater force and further additions. Like the good rhetoricians they are, they offer a point-for-point refutation of Crito's plea to escape. There is immense danger to friends; no good to be gained for Socrates' children; and threat to Socrates' existence as a free man. But their main question, perhaps, is, "Those arguments of yours about justice and the other virtues—what will they mean to us then?"

The speech concludes with a coda (54b-d). The Laws summarize their argument, and urge once again the primacy of justice in moral decision. In the course of their plea, they further hold that Socrates goes to his death the victim of injustice at the hands of men, not at the hands of the Laws themselves. If that were so, Socrates' escape would involve something more than returning injury for injury. It would involve injuring those who have not injured him.

Yet the claim may well seem disingenuous. Socrates was not convicted by men acting as men, but by men acting as jurymen and judges, that is, by men functioning in a legal capacity. Given that their administration of the law produced a wrong, why should not Socrates be described as a victim of law?

The reply to this question is direct, and drawn from the art analogy which Socrates introduced earlier in argument with Crito. A physician or a cobbler or a poet may make mistakes; but he makes them, not as a physician or cobbler or poet, but as a man. That is, he does not make mistakes in virtue of his art, but precisely in virtue of his failure to practice it (see *Republic* I 340c-341a, 342a-c). So too with judges, a point stressed by Socrates in the *Apology* (see 35b-c, 40a, 48d). Socrates was found guilty by men who held the office of dicasts or judges, but who did not function as judges because they were misled by their passions as men. This is a failure to which the application of law, like the application of any art, is liable—but not *as* law, nor *as* art.

This bears on a further point. The *Crito* assumes that given applications of law have the authority of law. It does not assume that law is to be identified with given applications. Socrates was not guilty of the charge of impiety for which he was condemned; but it is nowhere suggested that the law against impiety, as distinct from the verdict condemning him, is unjust. This aspect of the argument has been emphasized by Professor Jerome Hall:

The gist of Socrates' position comes to this: Athenian law is right law. But the specific application of such law to human affairs, the administration of law, the decisions and sentences, are sometimes erroneous and, therefore, unjust. But since laws can be applied only in particular decisions, these judgements must be obeyed even if they are unjust. Here, in Plato's separation of law from decisions is the origin of the theory, rejected in recent thinking, though not without important modern support, that law exists apart from specific decisions. . . .[44]

Law is distinct from its application if application may be unjust when the law applied is not, and if law is distinct from applications of law, it can hardly be said that law exists only in specific decisions—or their prediction. To identify the justice of law with the justice of given verdicts is to claim a self-certifying truth for verdicts which no human judgment, applied to contingent matters of fact, can claim. The personification of law in the *Crito* suggests, and the argument of the *Crito* itself assumes, that laws are things which are distinct from though not independent of the verdicts rendered according to them. If that were not so, the judge would be misnamed: with or without the divine afflatus, he is an oracle. But if decisions, as legal, involve the application of rules of law, and presuppose the existence of courts whose judgments are themselves made authoritative by law, then, so far from it being the case that law exists only in specific decisions, specific decisions, as legal, exist only in virtue of law—only in virtue of a legal order which contains as distinguishable elements the rules which courts apply and the rules which empower courts to apply them. There is in this, no doubt, an existential circle: the existence of a legal system implies its authority; its authority implies application of its rules; but authoritative application of its rules implies the existence of the legal system. There is no law without application; there is no application without law.

If this is so, the existence of a legal order is distinct from any body of rules, however complex. This is why it is consistent to acknowledge a duty of allegiance to the legal order, while rejecting given rules as unjust. If a law imposing criminal sanctions for impiety is right law, as Professor Hall insists, it by no means follows that corrupting the youth is impiety, or that Socrates criminally corrupted the youth by asking questions. No less surely than the unjust verdict, the failure of legality in the Athenian process was a failure of justice. But the argument implies that, up to the point where the legal system itself deserves to be destroyed, the rule that judgments judicially rendered are authoritative is authoritative.

Conclusion (54d-e)

Crito began by offering an argument from shame. The Laws of Athens have transposed that argument into a new key. In the *Apology* (28b), Socrates imagines someone asking him whether he does not feel ashamed at having pursued a course which has brought him to trial for his life; his reply is that the only thing a man should look to when he acts is whether his action is just or unjust (cf. *Crito* 49a-b). That question is not to be settled by taking votes, and does not depend on public opinion. It depends on discourse, reasoning, argument. The Laws have provided that argument, and the path of justice is clear. The dialogue ends on a note of quiet acceptance, with Socrates speaking again in his own voice, affirming the *logos* of the Laws.

Assumpsit

It is a curiosity of intellectual history that the argument of the *Crito* should have anticipated, without, surely, in any way having influenced, elements in the history of the development of informal contracts at common law. The argument of the *Crito* moves, not from a naked agreement which is then vested with some formal or informal requirement, but from an injury or detriment to the Laws of Athens occasioned by breach of a prior agreement. The argument, in short, is not purely contractual; it is delictual, but delictual as resting on a prior undertaking or agreement. Oddly enough, this structure matches with considerable precision the medieval writ of Assumpsit, which stands as an ancestor of the modern law of contract.

In the reign of the First Edward, three writs were available which provided what today would be regarded as contractual or quasi-contractual remedies: Covenant, for writing under seal; Debt, for wrongful retention of money; and Detinue, for wrongful retention of chattels. Debt and Detinue had as their central notion, not promising, but owing. Maitland's description of Debt applies to the sister-action of Detinue as well:

In its earliest stages the action is thought of as an action whereby a man 'recovers' what belongs to him. . . . It enters no one's head that a promise is the ground of this action. No pleader propounding such an action will think of beginning his count with 'Whereas the defendant promised to pay'; he will begin with 'Whereas the plaintiff lent or (as the case may be) sold or leased to the defendent'. In short, he will mention some *causa debendi* and that cause will not be a promise.[1]

One might say, for nutshell effect, that Debt and Detinue are actions for recovering what is owned by one man but in the possession of another. The procedure attached to the writs allowed compurgation.

Debt/Detinue gave no action for a promise broken or a promise badly kept. But then, we do promise, and so did our ancestors, and because we promise, we rely on promises, and rely on them sometimes to our injury. In the reign of the First Edward, no writ dealt with this except Covenant, which required that the promise be in writing and under seal; injurious reliance was irrelevant. The path of development in contract lay in a different direction. Specifically, it lay in what Maitland called "that fertile mother of actions," Trespass, an action which was rational in that its procedure required, not oath-helpers, but a finding of fact.

Trespass, *transgressionem vi et armis et contra pacem regis*, probably began as a civil action closely related to the appeals of felony.[2] Its basis was a wrong to the plaintiff in body, goods, or land, and a wrong done by force and arms and in breach of the king's peace. The action was limited in two significant ways. In the first place, if damage was claimed in Trespass, it had to be a direct and immediate result of the trespass; thus if you, clearing your field, threw a log into the road and struck your neighbor, intentionally or unintentionally, it was trespass, because the harm was direct and immediate; but if you left the log in the road and he later came and stumbled on it to his hurt, it was no trespass, whether you left it in a fit of absence of mind or in the cordial hope that he would come and break his neck. In the second place, touching goods and land, there could be no trespass unless there was possession; if you left your horse with a farrier to be shod or cured, and the farrier shod him so carelessly as to lame him or cured him so carelessly as to kill him, it was no trespass, because at the time of the harm you were not in possession of the horse; but if the harm occurred while you were holding the horse's bridle, it was trespass.

By the Second Statute of Westminster (13 Edw. I, c. 24 [1285]), the Chancery was authorized to issue new writs in circumstances similar (*in consimili casu*) to those already provided for, and whether as a result of the statute or as a clarification of what had come to be the growth of actual pleading, Trespass *vi et armis* came to be distinguished from Trespass on the case, or more simply, Case. In Case, the charge of force and arms, which had become increasingly formal, is dropped, and in its place there appears a stated ground of complaint: the complaint may claim indirect rather than direct damage, and damage based on ownership as distinct from possession. By the middle of the fourteenth century, Assumpsit appears as a kind of action on the case: someone undertakes (*assumpsit*) to do a certain thing, and does it so badly that harm rather than benefit results; he is now liable. The ferryman who undertook to carry your horse across the Humber and by overloading the boat drowned him, the farrier who undertook to shoe your horse and lamed him, must now answer at common law.[3]

Assumpsit is contractual in the sense that a prior undertaking is substantial to the action: no undertaking, *non assumpsit*. But the undertaking is important only because it is the occasion for the wrong: the action lies, not for breach of promise, but for damage done. In short, the primary theory of the action is not contractual but delictual; it is an action, not for a promise broken, but for a promise badly kept. The damage must result from a positive act, not an omission; it lies, not for not doing, but for not doing well:

The ferryman had of course failed to carry the mare over the river. But he was sued, not because it was left on the bank, but because it was dead. He was not naturally liable in covenant, any more than the borrower who damaged what he borrowed was liable in detinue. The complaint was not of failure to carry out the 'contractual' obligation, but of damage actually caused.[4]

Not until about 1500 will a pure omission become a recognized ground for an Assumpsit. The promisee will then have an action if he sustained loss as the result of a promise unperformed. The way is then open to claim that detriment to the promisee may arise simply from nonperformance, nonfeasance rather than misfeasance.

But we need not carry the story so far. Enough has been said to exhibit the similarity in structure between the argument of the *Crito* and the action of Assumpsit in its original form. The argument of the *Crito* turns on wrongful harm to the Laws of Athens resulting from a positive act, that of escape; Socrates' agreement to live as a citizen is substantial to that delict, in that it is a necessary condition for the wrongfulness of escape, just as a prior agreement was substantial to a charge of misfeasance in Assumpsit. And Socrates goes to his death, finally, not to avoid breaking a promise, but to avoid the doing of wrongful harm.

Legal Obligation in the *Crito*

Hobbes once remarked that in government, when nothing else is turned up, clubs are trumps. But in real life, which is not a game, clubs are no longer trumps when one is facing spades. If law consisted, as Professor Hart's excellent phrase has it, in "orders backed by threats,"[1] if the authority of law from the point of view of the citizen derived only from coercion, the issue discussed in the *Crito* could not arise. To suppose that a man ought to abide by his own death sentence because it has been decreed by law is to suppose, minimally, that the binding claim of law does not rest on force.

The *Crito* thus rules out a large and varied class of theories, ranging from Antiphon to Austin and Kelsen, which begin with the fact that law is usually accompanied by sanctions for the violation of its rules, and conclude that the coercion involved in legal sanctions is of the essence of legal authority. John Austin put the position vigorously:

Laws or rules, properly so called, are a species of commands. . . . If you express or intimate a wish that I shall do or forbear from some act, and if you will visit me with an evil in case I comply not with your wish, the expression or intimation of your wish is a command. . . . A command, then, is a signification of desire. But a command is distinguished from other significations of desire by this peculiarity: that the party to whom it is directed is liable to an evil from the other, in case he comply not with the desire. Being liable to an evil from you if I comply not with a wish you signify, I am bound or obliged by your command,

or I lie under a duty to obey it. If, in spite of that evil in prospect, I comply not
with the wish which you signify, I am said to disobey your command, or to vio-
late the duty which it imposes. Command and duty are, therefore, correlative
terms: the meaning denoted by each being implied or supposed by the other.[2]

The imperative theory of law, since coercion is morally neutral, implies legal positivism as a substantial claim about the content of a legal
system: it implies, that is, that law may have any content, or, in Austin's terms, that the existence of a law is one thing, its merit or demerit another. Here is the hidden identity between legal positivism
and anarchism. For the anarchist does not deny the social fact of a
coercive legal order, but rather denies that the legal order, as legal, has
moral authority to bind his conduct.

But the *Crito*, though much concerned about the authority of law,
does not locate that authority in the sanctions law imposes. The *Crito*
supposes that law retains its binding claim on conduct even when the
force which backs it has been exhausted through application; and the
very application of that force has itself a binding claim, not because
it is force, but because it is force of law. Sanctions imposed by a court,
even when unjust, are binding on citizens precisely because they pro-
ceed from law. But if citizens are bound to abide by the application
of sanctions because those sanctions are legal, the authority of law
does not derive from coercion, since the authority of coercion derives
from the authority of law. Put otherwise, the force exercised in the
application of legal sanctions is itself lawful force, and therefore force
or coercion cannot enter into the definition of legality.

Legal sanctions, though they may provide a motive for obedience
to law, are not an element in the analysis of legal obligation. To use
the language of the *Euthyphro* (11a), coercion is a *pathos* of legal obligation, not its *ousia*, something which generally accompanies legal
obligation and not an element in its nature or definition. The obligation which law imposes is moral: it rests on the contractual nature of
citizenship, and the wrongfulness of working injury.

The claim that law rests essentially on force is generally backed by
an appeal to fact. Thus, for example, Thrasymachus, when asked in
the *Republic* to define justice, claims that justice is the interest of the
stronger, and offers the following account in defense of his claim:

In every case, the laws are made by the ruling party in its own interest; a democracy makes democratic laws, a despot autocratic ones, and so on. By making
these laws they define as 'right' for their subjects whatever is in their own interest,
and they call anyone who breaks them a 'wrongdoer' and punish him accordingly.

That is what I mean: in all states alike 'right' has the same meaning, namely what is for the interest of the party in power, and that is the stronger. So the sound conclusion is that what is 'right' is the same everywhere: the interest of the stronger party. [*Republic* I 338e-339a, trans. Cornford]

The definition implies that legal authority is based on coercion, and, of course, that law may have any content. Thrasymachus backs his claim by a description of fact: he might have said, had he had the word in his vocabulary, that it was 'scientific'.[3] But there is a logical gap between description and definition. The fact, if it is a fact, that law is accompanied by force does not imply that force is *essential* to legal obligation, for the latter is a claim, not of fact, but of necessity.

If, as the *Crito* holds, the binding claim of law is moral, and does not rest on force, it is a tempting inference that it derives from coincidence with a set of objective moral rules fixed in the nature of things. Perhaps positive law—black-letter or, if you will, stone-chiselled law—binds because of its conformity with unwritten laws of natural justice. If that is so, positive law as *law* derives its warrant and authority from coincidence or consistency with natural law. Positive law as *positive* imposes no obligation which does not rest on force.

The natural law tradition is founded on the conflict, always possible within any legal system, between positive law and the requirements of morality. The mind of Sophocles, haunted by the conflict, gave it classic expression in the *Antigone*. Creon, Prince of Thebes, orders the body of Polyneices, a rebel, to be left unburied on pain of death, thus denying rest to the soul of the dead man and safe passage to the underworld. Antigone, sister of Polyneices, performs the forbidden funeral rites, thereby discharging as fundamental a duty to kindred as Greek morality knew. When brought before Creon she appeals to a higher law than his:

> It was not Zeus who issued me this order,
> Nor did that Justice which dwells with the nether Gods
> Establish laws of this sort among men.
> I did not think your edict of such force
> That you, a mortal, could trample underfoot
> The unwritten and immovable prescriptions of the Gods.
> Those prescriptions live, not now or yesterday, but always,
> And no man knows whence they have appeared.
> I was not willing, for fear of any man's intent,
> To render justice for their breach before the Gods.
> I knew that I must die. How could I not,

Even if you had not commanded it?
And if I die before my time, I count it gain.
Who would not count it gain who lives as I,
Encompassed by many evils?
But if I'd left my mother's son dead and unburied,
I'd now have cause to grieve as I grieve not. [lines 450-68]

A play is not a work of philosophy; Antigone is a passionate woman moved by a sister's love, not a lady jurisprude discoursing on the relation of law and theology. These lines express, not a theory, but a primitively felt response to a rending moral dilemma. It remained for Aristotle to generalize:

By two kinds of law I mean particular law and universal law. Particular law is that which each community lays down and applies to its own members: this is partly written and partly unwritten. Universal law is the law of nature. For there really is, as everyone to some extent divines, a natural justice and injustice that is binding on all men, even on those who have no association or covenant with each other. It is this that Sophicles' Antigone clearly means when she says that the burial of Polyneices was a just act in spite of the prohibition: she means that it was just by nature.[4]

For Aristotle, the principles of natural justice, as they apply to law, are the principles of social organization in its most developed form, exhibited by the well-run Greek city-state. But not long after Aristotle's death, Chrysippus took the further step of associating law with physics, on the ground that both are founded on Nature and Necessity: law is right reason derived from Zeus, commanding what is to be done and forbidding what is not to be done.[5] That definition passed from Greece to Rome,[6] from Rome to Europe, and crossed the Narrow Seas. Blackstone stretched his hand over the centuries, past the Publicists, past Cicero, to Chrysippus, and defined municipal law, the law of a single state or nation, as "a rule of civil conduct prescribed by the supreme power in a state, commanding what is right and prohibiting what is wrong." That rule of conduct, insofar as it deals not with mere *mala prohibita* but *mala in se*, derives from the law of nature and of nature's God:

This law of nature, being coeval with mankind and dictated by God himself, is of course superior in obligation to any other. It is binding all over the globe, in all countries, and at all times; no human laws are of any validity, if contrary to this; and such of them as are valid derive all their force, and all their authority, mediately or immediately, from this original.[7]

Blackstone offers an account of sovereignty which anticipates that of John Austin. He differs from Austin in supposing that positive law gains its binding claim solely from natural law, and that positive law is declarative of natural rights and duties. In short, positive law gains its moral warrant from natural law, and a law contrary to natural law is not law.

Whatever the merits of this view, it is not the view of the *Crito*. The *Crito* neither states nor implies that an unjust law is not law, nor that law derives its binding claim from a content which coincides with principles of natural justice. On the contrary, the *Crito* explicitly allows that given laws, like given verdicts, may differ from what is by nature just (51c), and that they may be incorrect or ill-directed (50d, 51e). Yet the citizen is under obligation to obey those laws, unless he can alter them by persuasion rather than force (51b-c). This obligation, it will be observed, is to law as law, not to law as coinciding with a given moral content. The Laws of Athens make their claim on Socrates because they are the laws of *Athens,* a city of which he is a citizen, not because they are images or derivatives of some universal law which lies beyond them. The very laws of Hades are described, not as parents, but as brothers—coordinate laws applying in a different jurisdiction (cf. 54c). The binding claim of law in the *Crito* is the claim of positive law: positive law *as* positive, the actually existing law of a given municipal system.

The force of this point, as well as the danger of too facile an appeal to a law beyond positive law—a standard device of Greek pleading[8]—is brought out by Arginusae, when the ten generals (or admirals—a *strategos* went to sea) were tried for failing to gather up the dead for burial. It happened that Socrates was president of the Prytanate on this occasion,[9] charged with the duty of deciding what issues should be brought to vote; he refused to put the question on grounds of illegality, and was overriden. He condemns the proceedings as unjust, and rests his claim, not on the substantive issue of guilt or innocence, but on the fact that it involved violating a procedural safeguard of Athenian law: the safeguard, namely, that men who must die as individuals shall not be tried and condemned as a group. It is, of course, peculiarly legal to rest a question of justice on a question of procedure; and if it is suggested that the observance of procedural safeguards is not only a legal but moral duty, it is to be observed that this particular moral duty presupposes the existence of positive law. The point, indeed, runs deeper. If the binding claim of positive law rested solely on its justice, then positive law would cease to bind when misapplied. Socrates, being wrongfully condemned for impiety, would have a right to escape. The *Crito*, on the contrary, maintains that he is under a duty not to escape, and the existence of that duty rests squarely on the authority of positive law.

Few documents in the history of western legal and moral philosophy have pitched the obligations of citizenship so high, and the argument, whatever its felt cogency, may well produce a sense of discomfort and doubt. There is reason in this. The *Crito* does not raise the question, which was not less pressing in fifth-century Athens than it is today, of the possibility of conflict between a man's duties as a citizen and his duties as a man. One need not range afield for examples. It is only necessary to juxtapose the *Crito* and the *Apology*—remembering that behind the *Apology* lies the heritage of the *Antigone*.

The *Crito* maintains that:

The just lies here: never to give way, never to desert, never to leave your post, but in war or court of law or any other place, to do what City and Country command—that, or to persuade it of what is by nature just. It is not holy to use force against a mother or father; and it is far more unholy to use force against your country than against them. [51b-c]

Compare the *Apology*:

I should indeed have wrought a fearful thing, Gentlemen of Athens, if, when the commanders you chose stationed me at Potidaea and Amphipolis and Delium, I remained where I was stationed, as others did, and ran the risk of death; but when it was the God who stationed me, as I thought and believed, obliging me to live in the pursuit of wisdom, examining myself and others—if then, at that point, through fear of death or any other thing, I left my post. [28d-29a]

If the court were to offer Socrates a release on the condition that he cease his inquiry at the behest of the God, he would refuse it:

If, as I say, you were to dismiss me on that condition, I would reply that I hold you in friendship and esteem, Gentlemen of Athens, but I shall obey the God rather than you, and so long as I have breath and am able I shall not cease to pursue wisdom or to exhort you. [30d]

Obedience to the God rather than Athens. Yet in the *Crito*, obedience to lawful authority is itself a matter of holiness and divine apportionment (51b). And if it is suggested that the *Crito* allows for persuasion of the law to what is by nature right, it may be observed that the situation envisaged in the *Apology* is one in which such persuasion is or may be itself forbidden by law.

Again, take the story of Socrates and the Thirty Tyrants, and the order to bring back Leon from Salamis for judicial murder (*Apology* 32c-d). Socrates refused to obey an unjust command. Did he not, in the name of justice, refuse to obey lawful authority? And was his action not therefore, by the standards of the *Crito*, itself unjust? It may be argued that the Thirty were usurpers, and their decrees not legally binding. As a historical matter, it is by no means clear that this is true. And leaving aside the extent of their wrongs, the kind of action they commanded was not impossible under the radical democracy which preceded the oligarchy in Athens, nor in the restored democracy, moderate in most respect though it was, which sentenced Socrates to death. Can there be any doubt that, had such a command issued from lawfully constituted authority, Socrates would still have gone home?

There is, after all, an analogy between Antigone's defiance of Creon and Socrates' conduct in Athens. He has pursued his mission to Athens at the behest of the God at Delphi, and he will refuse to give over, whatever the consequences. As he was stationed by his commanders at Potidaea, Amphipolis, and Delium, there to run the risk of wounds and death, so he has been stationed by the God to live in the pursuit of wisdom, examining both himself and others (*Apology* 28d-29a). If the court were to offer him release on the condition that he cease his inquiry, he would refuse because of his service to the God (30d), as he refused to take part in a judicial murder at the behest of the Thirty. The *Apology* is very like the philosopher's *Antigone*.

But the metaphor of the good soldier recurs in the *Crito* with what appears to be precisely opposite force. The just lies here: never to yield, never to desert, never to leave one's post, but in war or court of law or anything else to do what City and Country command (51b-c). The *Crito* in its relation to the *Apology* poses a problem of interpretation. In the *Apology*, obedience to the God rather than Athens. Yet in the *Crito*, obedience to lawful authority is itself a matter of holiness and divine apportionment (51b). And if it is suggested that the *Crito* allows of persuasion of the law to what is by nature just, the situation envisaged in the *Apology* is one in which such persuasion is or may be forbidden by law. Bentham's suggestion that the good citizen will obey punctually and criticize freely begs an important question.

If the collocation of the *Apology* and the *Crito* poses a problem of interpretation, it also points to a paradox which is fundamental to jurisprudence and its intersection with moral theory. In conjunction, the *Apology* and *Crito* appear to assume the following propositions:

i) Positive law imposes a moral obligation on citizens for obedience.

ii) Positive law—rule, verdict, judgment, edict, decree—may forbid what is right or require what is wrong.

It seems a direct inference from (i) and (ii) that,

iii) A citizen may be obligated to do or forbear from doing what he is obligated not to do or forbear from doing.

In short, if you claim that there is an obligation to obey the law, and claim also that given laws or their administration may be unjust, in that they may require what is wrong, then you appear committed to the result that, on occasion, you ought to do what you ought not to do. It will be observed that (iii) involves a contradiction, since, though it does not follow that if someone is not under an obligation to do X he is under an obligation not to do X, it follows *ex vi terminorum* that if someone is under an obligation not to do X he is not under an obligation to do X. To deny this would be to remove consistency as a criterion of moral discourse. If moral judgments are capable of being true or false, or if moral reasoning is to be possible, in the sense of allowing passage from premises to conclusion, consistency must abide.

The paradox is not peculiar to the interpretation of the *Crito*: it is a touchstone in the philosophy of law. Because (iii) is contradictory, either it does not follow from (i) and (ii) or (i) and (ii) cannot without qualification both be true. Theories of natural law of the Blackstonian rather than Calliclean persuasion generally accept (i) and reject (ii): given that there is a moral obligation to obey positive law, a claim which this tradition has great difficulty in explaining, law which requires the doing of injustice is not law, and imposes no obligation to obedience. To this there is an obvious objection, for as a factual matter, the law that is *is* law, being what judges and lawyers, legislators and assemblymen, apply, argue, and make. Again, as a matter of fact, the law that is is sometimes unjust.

It is on the latter point that legal positivism takes its stand. To claim that unjust law is not law, it is said, confuses law as it is with law as it ought to be; the truth is that the existence of a law is one thing and its merit or demerit another. John Austin, in an endnote to lecture 5 of *The Province*, criticized Blackstone on this point with remarkable directness:

To say that human laws which conflict with the Divine law are not binding, that is to say, are not laws, is to talk stark nonsense. The most pernicious laws, and therefore those which are most opposed to the will of God, have been and are continually enforced by judicial tribunals. . . . An exception, demurrer, or plea, founded on the law of God was never heard in a Court of Justice, from the creation of the world down to the present moment.

As a historical matter, Austin is mistaken. Aristotle's *Rhetoric* was, among other things, a descriptive manual of Greek trial practice, and the distinction between particular and universal law was a commonplace of advocacy.[10] In Austin's own country today, defect of natural justice is a reason for granting *certiorari* or declaratory judgment,[11] and courts retain a much-debated common law power to declare immoral acts criminal, as in *Shaw's Case*.[12] But as an analytic matter, Austin might reply that the reasons given for a judgment must be distinguished from the jurisprudential basis on which the judgment is given, and may follow on considerations extrinsic to the nature of law. Laws are imperatives. The nature of law is to be analyzed in terms of the obligation it imposes, and the obligation it imposes is to be analyzed in terms of coercion. A legal duty is the reflex of an expressed wish and a conditional penalty.

This yields a simple solution to the paradox of legal obligation: the paradox rests on an equivocation between legal and moral duty. It is tautological to say that there is a legal obligation to obey the law because it is the law, given that law is essentially a command. It is contradictory to say that positive law may be legally unjust, if that means that it does not impose a legal duty. And it is not a contradiction, but simple truth, to say that a man may be legally obligated to do what he is morally obligated not to do. As John Chipman Gray put it, "If legal duties are the acts and forbearances which an organized society will compel, it is obvious that many very immoral acts and forebearances have been legal duties."[13]

The positivist likes to present himself as a tough-minded thinker inspecting the depths of legal space with clear and unwavering eye; he has frequent occasion to take dim views of his brethren in the Blackstonian tradition, who stand in outer darkness confusing the Ought with the Is. One might truly wish it were all so simple. There is, indeed, no contradiction in claiming that one may be legally obligated to do what one is morally obligated not to do, or vice versa. But if this resolves inconsistency at the level of statement, it hardly does so at the level of action. Both law and morality provide a rule for conduct, and if one rule forbids what the other permits or requires, there is practical incompatibility and the agent must choose. The distinction between legal oughts and moral oughts is otiose: there is only an ought. Austin's account of obligation rests on a bad pun, for coercion does not imply duty.[14] So far as the *Crito* is concerned, the case is clear: the obligation of law cannot be defined in terms of legal sanctions, if acceptance of the sanction is itself an obligation of law. If

Austin were correct in supposing that coercion is an element in the definition of legal obligation, the account of legal obligation in the *Crito* would be, not false, but either logically false or meaningless.

It remains to show that the premises of the *Crito*, so far from implying the absurdity of (iii), preclude it. To begin with, (iii) does not follow from (i) and (ii), because the syllogism contains four terms. Proposition (i) is true because 'law' means the legal order, taken collectively; the moral obligation of the citizen is fidelity to law in the *Crito*—obey the law, or accept the consequences of not obeying. Proposition (ii) is true because 'law' means the legal order taken distributively: given laws may indeed be unjust. Proposition (iii) follows from (i) and (ii) in the same way that 'Oscar is numerous' follows from the fact that mice are numerous and Oscar is a mouse.

The premises of the *Crito*, in fact, preclude (iii). If one ought never do injustice, one ought not do injustice when the laws command it.[15] If one ought to abide by agreements when it is just to do so, and one ought never do injustice, it must follow that a binding agreement cannot require the doing of injustice. Given that voluntary acceptance of citizenship implies a binding agreement, the doing of injustice at the behest of law is no part of its terms, and a law or decree which requires a citizen to do injustice is, for that citizen, in some strict sense *ultra vires*. No agreement can lend it authority, and specifically not the agreement to live as a citizen.[16] Because this is so, to refuse to obey a law or decree which requires one to do injustice is not to injure the law; for injury arises only from breach of authority, and authority extends only so far as agreement binds. The *Crito* is in fact quite consistent with the *Apology*. Socrates was not under an obligation to take part in a judicial murder, by whatever government ordered, because it would have involved the doing of injustice. He was not under obligation to obey Athens rather than the God, because this would have involved the specific form of injustice which is impiety (see *Gorgias* 507a-b). The *Crito*'s claim that positive law imposes a moral obligation to obedience, in short, is true only under a restriction—a restriction inherent in the premises by which the argument proceeds.

But it is well to recognize that the scope of the restriction is limited. It holds for the *doing* of injustice. It does not hold for the *suffering* of it. To do injustice is to harm the soul. No such consequence attaches to the suffering of it, which can undoubtedly harm the body, but cannot harm the soul unless injustice is returned for injustice. "There is no evil for a good man either in living or dying, and the Gods do not neglect his affairs" (*Apology* 41d). Because the injustice involved in a mistaken verdict is one to which every application of law is liable, it falls within the terms of Socrates' implied agreement to abide by the decisions of courts. In abiding by that decision, Socrates' body will suffer harm—lethal harm. But Socrates' body is not Socrates. The alternative of escape implies harm to the soul, since it involves breach of a valid agreement and, thereby, injury to laws—involves, in short, the doing of injustice.

It is a foreseeable consequence of agreeing to live as a citizen and abide by the decisions of courts that courts will sometimes enforce laws which require the doing of injustice; and since the suffering of injustice at the hands of courts does not invalidate the agreement of citizenship, refusal to accept punishment involves injury to the laws and the doing of injustice. In short, one may be morally obligated to accept legal punishment for not doing what one was morally obligated not to do—once again, a paradox the Many will never accept. The argument of the *Crito*, taken in conjunction with the *Apology*, illustrates the point: Socrates held himself under an obligation not to disobey the God, and under an obligation to accept a sentence of death for refusing that disobedience. Law and sanction are detachable. One may be obligated to accept punishment for not doing what one was under an obligation not to do—once again, a paradox the Many will never accept.

The universalization principle on which the *Crito*'s argument turns implies a principle of what may be called legal validity: breach of *this* verdict is destructive of *all* law precisely because the verdict issued from a source legally empowered to render it. But validity may pertain to a law or decree requiring the doing of injustice quite as much as to a verdict requiring the suffering of it. Since that is so, refusal to do injustice at the behest of law would seem to be quite as much an injury to the legal order as refusal to suffer it. We are back to the absurdity of (iii).

But the answer is here as it was before. If one element in the analysis of legal authority is validity, the other is scope, and scope rests on binding agreement. No agreement can bind to the doing of injustice, and where no agreement binds, no authority exists. But where no authority exists, refusal to obey is no injury to law. Law, to be authoritative, must be valid. It by no means follows and is false to suppose that valid law is therefore in all cases authoritative. Validity is a necessary condition for authority, not a sufficient condition. Validity is a specifically legal concept. Authority is a moral concept which contains validity as an element in its analysis.

This, then, is the trick of perspective in the argument of the *Crito*. The argument turns on the law that judgments judicially rendered are authoritative; but more fundamentally, it turns on the principle that the law that judgments judicially rendered are authoritative is authoritative. The *Crito* provides an account of legal authority from the perspective, not only of the law, but of the citizen facing the law. From the latter point of view, the authority of law rests on the wrongfulness of doing injury, and the rightness of abiding by agreements. The authority of law is therefore conceptually distinguishable, and may in practice be distinct, from the claim of given laws to authority.

The *Crito* supposes that laws may be ill-directed or at variance with what is by nature just, and yet still bind to obedience up to the point where they require the doing of injustice. The reason is not far to seek. Laws are not merely rules, they are rules with an aim, and that aim is the good of the city and its citizens: the art of the statesman or lawgiver is akin to every other art in this respect, that, "Any kind of rule [*arche*] must, in its character of rule, consider solely what is best for those under its care" (*Republic* I 345d). But the achievement of aim admits of degree. Lawgivers, like other men, may mistake apparent good for real good; the statesman, like the practitioner of other arts, may make mistakes—though not in virtue of his art. Between the extremes of those laws which are precisely fitted to their aim and those laws which, because they require the doing of injustice, forfeit their authority, there is a large and varied range of possibilities. Socrates found much in the laws of Athens imperfect, and in many passages of the early dialogues is unsparing in his criticism of them. The argument of the *Crito* does not rest on false idealization. But up to the point where the laws required him to do injustice, Socrates supposed that they were to be obeyed or persuaded to what is by nature just—if necessary, at the cost of life itself.

To conclude. The *Crito* maintains that legal obligation rests essentially neither on force nor on a set of rules fixed in the nature of things or the mind of God. It maintains that fidelity to the legal order is a moral obligation, and of such weight as to require Socrates to abide by an unjust sentence of death. This conclusion is defended by argument, an argument which rests on the two premises that one ought not return injustice for injustice or injury for injury, and that one ought to abide by agreements, given that they are just. These two premises are combined with an account of legal authority which assumes, first, that Socrates by voluntarily assuming the status of citizenship has thereby entered into an implied agreement to abide by the decisions of courts, and second, that escape would constitute an injury to the law and the common constitution of Athens. The latter claim rests on a universalization principle: to act in breach of any given verdict is by so much to act in breach of all law, and thereby to injure the laws and encompass the destruction of the City. The premises of the *Crito*, however, imply a restriction in the following respect: the authority of law extends only so far as agreement binds, and though agreement will bind to the suffering of injustice, it cannot bind to the doing of it.

The premises of injury and agreement are intimately connected. The claim that Socrates will injure the Laws if he escapes implies that he stands within the scope of their authority, and this is true because of his agreement to live as a citizen. On the other hand, because his agreement brings him within the scope of authority of the laws, escape will constitute an injury to them. The *Crito* does not, as has often been thought, present a series of independent arguments for the conclusion that it is wrong to escape. It presents one argument with two interlocking premises. It is the premise of injury, however, not the premise of agreement, which is primary: for it is on the wrongfulness of doing injury or injustice that the weight of the argument rests.

If this account of the *Crito* is true, it may be contrasted with a more usual one, neatly summed up by Hume at the conclusion of his essay, "Of the Original Contract":

The only passage I meet with in antiquity, where the obligation of obedience to government is ascribed to a promise, is in Plato's *Crito*; where Socrates refused to escape from prison, because he had tacitly promised to obey the laws. Thus he builds a *Tory* consequence of passive obedience on a *Whig* foundation of the original contract.

But the *Crito*, though it establishes no right of revolution where citizenship is the result of voluntary agreement, and is thus not Whiggish, hardly recommends passive obedience.[17] Nor does the obligation of obedience to law rest simply on a promise. Socrates goes to his death because he has, by agreeing to live as a citizen, brought himself within the scope of legal authority, and because action in breach of that authority constitutes an injury to law. It is a curiosity of intellectual history that this structure of argument should match with considerable precision the medieval writ of Assumpsit at common law, a main ancestor of the modern law of contract.

The argument of the *Crito* rests on a revolution in morals, and issues in paradox. We are sometimes told that this new morality must satisfy the claims of popular morality. If it did, it would be inconsistent, but not paradoxical. Men acting by the standards of popular morality condemned Socrates to death for impiety; another man, acting by the same standards, urged him to escape. At the level of principle, popular morality was many things, not one. At the level of rules, it was at best a container requiring further content. Do not steal. Do not murder. Do not commit adultery. But theft is wrongful taking, murder wrongful killing, adultery wrongful intercourse—and in what does wrongfulness consist? One way of answering that question is by appeal to law; unless justice requires otherwise, the citizen owes obedience to law, and since there are many who will never discover for themselves what justice requires, it is by so much the more important that the laws be good. It is no accident that the Socratic legacy, in Plato's hands, issued in a school of jurisprudence. But the criterion of wrongfulness lies ultimately not in any set of rules, however skillfully framed, but in a single self-consistent standard of justice, an Idea fixed in the nature of things, by which the worth of rules, and all else, is to be estimated, and whose use is essential to human excellence, which is based on knowledge and allied to art.

Socrates never claimed to have attained certain knowledge of that standard. The man who in the *Apology* knew only that he did not know does not in the *Crito* lay claim to full knowledge of justice and virtue. The *Crito* presents, not demonstration, but dialectic, with the provisional quality which dialectic entails. But when dialectic has been carried through as far as possible and when such degree of clarity has been attained as human limitation permits, one must act—act on the conclusions that appear true. This conception of human rationality, lofty in its aim, is tentative and modest in its estimate of attainment. But in its insistence on the sovereignty of reason, it is immodest in its rejection of the contrary view: the view, namely, that reason is, and of a right ought to be, only the slave of the passions.

The Crito

43a Socrates. Why have you come at this hour, Crito? Isn't it still
early?

Crito. Very early.

S. What time, exactly?

C. Depth of dawn, before first light.

S. I'm surprised the guard was willing to admit you.

C. He's used to me by this time, Socrates, because I keep coming here so often. Besides, I've done him a kindness.

S. Did you come just now, or a while ago?

C. Quite a while ago.

b S. Then why didn't you wake me immediately, instead of sitting there in silence?

C. No, Socrates. I might wish I weren't in such wakeful pain myself, and I've been marvelling for some time at how sweetly you sleep. I didn't wake you on purpose, so that you could spend the time as pleasantly as possible. Often before through the whole of our lives I've thought you happy in your ways, but never more than now in the present misfortune—so cheerfully and lightly do you bear it.

c S. But surely, Crito, it would scarcely be appropriate in a man of my age to be distressed if he now had to die.

C. Other men as old have been taken in similar misfortune, Socrates, and age did not relieve their distress at what had come.

115

S. True. But why are you here so early?

C. I bring grievous news, Socrates. Not grievous to you, it appears, but grievous to me and to all your companions, and heaviest to bear, I think, for me.

d   S. What is it? Has the ship come from Delos, on whose arrival I'm to die?

C. Not yet. But I think it will come today, to judge from the report of some people who've arrived from Sunium and left it there. From what they say, it will clearly come today, and then tomorrow, Socrates, your life must end.

S. Well, Crito, let it be for the best. If so it pleases the Gods, let it be so. Still, I don't think it will come today.

44a   C. From what do you infer that?

S. I'll tell you. I'm to die, I think, the day after the ship arrives.

C. Yes—so the authorities say, at any rate.

S. Then I think it will come tomorrow, not today. I infer that from a dream I saw a little while ago tonight. Perhaps you chose a good time not to wake me.

C. What was the dream?

S. A woman appeared to me. She came, fair and beautiful of

b   form, clothed in white, and she called to me and said, "Socrates, on the third day shalt thou go to fertile Phthia."

C. A strange dream, Socrates.

S. But Crito, I think a clear one.

C. Yes, too clear, it seems.

Crito's Exhortation to Escape

C. But please, Socrates, my beloved friend, please let me persuade you even at this point. Save yourself. As for me, if you should die it will be a multiple misfortune. Quite apart from the loss of such friendship as I shall not find again, people who don't really know us will think I didn't care,

c   because I could have saved you if only I'd been willing to spend the money. Yet what could be more shameful, than the appearance of putting money before friends? People won't believe that you refused to escape even though we were eager to help.

S. But Crito, why should we be concerned about what people will think? Those worth considering will believe that things happened as they did.

d   C. Surely at this point, Socrates, you see how necessary it really is to care about what people think. The very things now happening show that they can accomplish, not the least of evils, but very nearly the greatest, if a man has been slandered among them.

S. If only they could work the greatest evils, Crito, so that they might also work the greatest goods, it would truly be well. But as it is, they can do neither: they cannot make a man wise or foolish. They only act at random.

e   C. Very well, let that be so. But tell me this, Socrates. Are you worried about me and the rest of your friends? Are you afraid that, if you escape, the sycophants will make trouble for us for helping you, so that we may be compelled to forfeit our estates or a great deal of money, or suffer more besides? If you're afraid of something of that sort, dismiss it.

45a   It is right for us to run that risk to save you, and still greater risk if need be. Please, let me persuade you to do as I say.

S. Of course I'm worried about those things, Crito, and many other things too.

C. Then don't be afraid. In fact, it's not a large sum which certain people are willing to take to manage your escape, and as for the sycophants, you see how cheaply they can be bought; it wouldn't take much money for them. You have

b   mine at your disposal, and it is, I think, enough, but if you're somehow worried about me and think you shouldn't spend mine, your friends from abroad are ready.[1] One of them, Simmias of Thebes, has brought enough money just for the purpose, and Cebes and quite a few others are ready, too. So as I say, you mustn't hesitate because of that. Nor should you be troubled about what you said in court, how if you went into exile you wouldn't know what to do with

c   yourself. There are many places for you to go where they'd welcome you warmly, but if you want to go to Thessaly, I have friends there who will honor and protect you, so that no one will cause you distress.

Furthermore, Socrates, I think the thing you're doing is wrong. You betray yourself when you could be saved. You hasten a thing for yourself of a kind your very enemies might hasten for you—and have hastened, wishing you destroyed. In addition, I think you're betraying your sons.

d   You desert them when you could raise and educate them;

so far as you're concerned, they're to take what comes, and what is likely to come is just what usually comes to orphans in the poverty of their orphanhood. No. Either a man shouldn't have children, or he should accept the burden of raising and educating them; the choice you're making is one of the most heedless indifference. Your choice should be that of a good and courageous man—especially since you say you've had a life-long concern for virtue. I'm ashamed,

e Socrates, ashamed both for you and for your friends, because it's going to seem that the whole business was done through a kind of cowardice in us. The case was brought to court when it needn't have been. Then there was the conduct of the trial. And now, as the final absurdity of the whole affair, it is to look as if we let slip this final opportunity because of our own badness and cowardice. These

46a things are bad, at once shameful to you and to us. Decide. Or rather at this hour, it isn't time to decide but to have decided. This is the last chance, because everything must be done this coming night, and if we wait it won't any longer be possible. Please, Socrates, be persuaded by me and do as I ask.

Socrates' Reply to Crito

b S. My dear Crito, your eagerness is worth much, if rightly directed. But if not, the greater it is, the worse. We must consider carefully whether this thing is to be done, for I am now and always have been the sort of man who is persuaded only by the argument which on reflection proves best to me, and I cannot throw over arguments I formerly accepted merely

c because of what has come; they still seem much the same, and I honor them as I did before. If we can't find better ones, I will not give way to you, not even if the power of the multitude were far greater than it now is, to frighten us like children with its threats of confiscation, bonds, and death.

Now, how might we most fairly consider the matter? Perhaps we should first take up this argument of yours

d about beliefs. We often used to say that some beliefs are worth paying attention to and others not. Was that wrong? Or was it right before I had to die, whereas it is now obviously idle nonsense put for the sake of arguing? I'd like to join with you in common inquiry, Crito. Does that appear in any way changed now that I'm here? Let us dismiss it or be persuaded by it. We often used to say, I think—and we used to think it made sense—that among the beliefs men entertain, some are to be regarded as important and others are not. Before the Gods, Crito, were we wrong? At least insofar as it lies in human agency, you aren't about to die tomorrow, and the present situation won't distort your judgment. So consider the matter. Don't you think it's satisfactory to say that one shouldn't value the beliefs of every man, but of some men and not others, and that one shouldn't value every belief of men, but some beliefs and not others? Isn't that right?

C. It is.

S. Now, it's useful beliefs which should be valued, not harmful or bad ones?

C. Yes.

S. Useful ones being those of the wise, bad ones those of the foolish?

C. Of course.

S. To continue, what did we used to say about things like this. Suppose a man goes in for atheletics. Does he pay attention to the opinions, the praise and blame, of everybody, or only the one man who is his physician or trainer?

C. Only the one.

S. Then he ought to welcome the praise and fear the blame of that one man, not the multitude.

C. Clearly.

S. So he is to train and exercise, eat and drink, in a way that seems good to a supervisor who knows and understands, rather than anyone else.

C. True.

S. Very well. But if he disobeys that supervisor, scorns his judgment, values the judgment of the multitude who are without understanding, won't he suffer an evil?

C. Of course.

S. What is that evil? Whither does it tend, and into what possession of the man who disobeys?

C. Into the body, clearly, for it ruins that.

S. Right. And isn't this also true in other matters, Crito? We don't need to run through them all, but isn't it specifically true of what is just and unjust, honorable and shameful, good and evil—just the things our decision is now concerned with? Are we to fear and follow the multitiude in such mat-

d   ters? Or is it rather the opinion of one man, if he but have knowledge, which we must reverence and fear beyond all the rest, since if we do not follow it, we'll permanently damage and corrupt something we used to say becomes better by justice and is harmed by injustice. Or is there no such thing?

C. I certainly think there is, Socrates.

S. Very well then, suppose that, by disobeying the opinion of those who understand, we were to ruin what becomes better by health and is damaged by disease. Would life be worth

e   living for us once it has been damaged? That is the body, of course.

C. Yes.

S. Well, would life be worth living with a wretched, damaged body?

C. Surely not.

S. Then is it worth living when there is damage to what the just benefits and the unjust corrupts? Or do we think that

48a   this—whatever it is of ours to which justice and injustice pertain—is of less worth than the body?

C. Surely not.

S. Of more worth?

C. Far more.

S. Then perhaps we shouldn't give much thought to what the multitude tells us, my friend. Perhaps we should rather think of what he will say who understands things just and unjust—he being but one man, and the very Truth itself. So your first claim, that we ought to pay attention to what the multitude thinks about what is just and honorable and good, is mistaken. "But then," someone might say, "the multitude can kill us."

b   C. Yes, Socrates, it is very clear someone might say that. You're right.

S. And yet, my friend, the conclusion we've reached still seems much as it did before. Then too, consider whether this agreement still abides too: that it is not living which is of most importance, but living well.

C. It does.

S. But 'well' is the same as honorably and justly—does that abide too?

C. Yes.

S. Then in light of these arguments, we must consider whether it would be right for me to try to escape without permission of the Athenians. If it proves right, let's try; if not, let's dismiss the matter. But as for these other considerations you raise about loss of money and raising children and what people think—Crito, those are really fit topics for people who lightly kill and would raise to life again without a thought if they could—the multitude. As for us, the argument has chosen: there's nothing to be considered but the things we've already mentioned—whether it is right to give

d money with our thanks to those who are going to manage my escape, whether it is right to escape or assist in it, or whether in actual fact we shall do injustice by doing any of these things. If it proves to be unjust, then perhaps we should give thought neither to death nor to anything else except the doing of injustice.

C. You are right, Socrates. Look to what we should do.

S. Let's examine the matter together, my friend, and if you can somehow refute what I'm going to say, do so, and I'll

e be convinced. But if not, then please, my dear friend, please stop returning over and over again to the same argument about how I ought to escape from here without permission from the Athenians. For I count it important that I act with your agreement, not against your will. So look to the starting

49a point of the inquiry. See whether it is satisfactorily stated, and try to answer what I ask as you think proper.

C. I'll certainly try.

Two Premises

S. Do we say that there are any circumstances in which injustice ought willingly or wittingly be done? Or is injustice to be done in some circumstances but not others? Is the doing of injustice in no way honorable or good, as we often in the past agreed, or have those former agreements been cast aside these last few days? Has it long escaped our notice,

b Crito, that as old men in serious discussion with each other

we were really no better than children, or is it rather precisely as we used to claim: that whether the multitude
agrees or not, whether we must suffer things still worse than
this or things more easy to bear, still, the doing of injustice
is in every circumstance shameful and evil for him who does
it. Do we affirm that, or not?

C. We do.

S. Then one must never do injustice.

C. Of course not.

S. Nor return injustice for injustice, as the multitude think,
since one must never do injustice.

c   C. That follows.

S. Then does this? Ought one work injury, Crito?

C. No, surely not, Socrates.

S. Then is it just to work injury in return for having suffered
it, as the multitude affirms?

C. Not at all.

S. No, for surely there is no difference between doing ill to
men and doing injustice.

C. True.

S. Then one ought not return injustice for injustice or do ill
to any man, no matter what one may suffer at their hands.

d   Look to this, Crito. Do not agree against your real opinion,
for I know that few men think or will ever think it true. Between those who accept it and those who do not, there is
no common basis for decision: when they view each others'
counsels, they must necessarily hold each other in contempt.
So consider very carefully whether you unite with me in
agreeing that it can never be right to do injustice or return
it, or to ward off the suffering of evil by doing it in return,
or whether you recoil from this starting point. I have long
thought it true and do still. If you think otherwise, speak

e   and instruct me. But if you abide by our former agreements,
hear what follows.

C. I do abide. Please go on.

S. I say next, or rather, I ask, whether one is to do things he
agreed with someone to do, given that they are just, or is
one to deceive?

C. One is to do them.

S. Then observe what follows. If I escape from here without

50a   persuading the City, am I not injuring someone, and someone I *least* ought? And am I not failing to abide by agreements it is just to keep?

C. Socrates, I can't answer what you ask, for I don't understand what you mean.

The Speech of the Laws of Athens

S. Look at it this way. Suppose I was about to run off from here, or whatever the thing should be called. And suppose the Laws, the common constitution of the City, came and stood before me and said, "Tell us, Socrates, what you intend to do. Do you mean by this to undertake to destroy us? To destroy, as far as in you lies, the Laws and the City as a whole? Or do you think that a city can any longer exist and not be overturned, in which legal judgments once rendered are without force, but may be rendered unauthoritative by private citizens and so corrupted.

How are we to answer that, Crito, and questions like it? A good deal might be said, especially by an orator, in behalf of that law, now to be broken, which requires that judgments judicially rendered be authoritative. Or are we to reply that the City did us an injustice and didn't decide the case correctly. Is that what we're to say?

C. Most emphatically, Socrates.

S. Then what if the Laws were to reply, "Socrates, was that really our agreement? Or was it rather to abide by such judgments as the City might render?" Now, if I were surprised at the question, they might go on, "There's no reason for surprise, Socrates. Answer the question, especially since you're so used to questions and answers. Come then, what charge do you lay against us and the City, that you should undertake to destroy us? We gave you birth. It was through us that your father took your mother to wife and begot you. Tell us, then, those of us here who are the Laws of Marriage, do you find some fault in us for being incorrect?"

"No fault," I would say.

"Then what about the Laws governing the rearing of children once born, and their education—the Laws under which you were in fact educated. Did we who are the Laws established for that purpose prescribe incorrectly when we e   directed your father to educate you in music and gymnastic?"[2]

"Correctly," I'd say.

"Very well, then. We bore you, reared you, educated you. Can you then say, first of all, that you are not our offspring and our slave—you, and your fathers before you? And if that's true, do you think that justice is on a level between you and us—that it is right for you to do in return what we may undertake to do to you? Was there such an equal balance toward your father, or your master if you happened to have one, so that you might return whatever was done
51a   to you—strike back when struck, speak ill when spoken ill to, things like that? Does such a possibility then exist toward your Country and its Laws, so that if we should undertake to destroy you, believing it right, you in return will undertake so far as you are able to destroy us, your Country and its Laws? Will you claim that this is right—you, who are so profoundly concerned about virtue? Or are you so wise that you've let it escape your notice that Country is to be honored beyond mother and father or any forebears; that
b   it is more holy, more to be revered, of greater apportionment among both gods and men of understanding; that an angered Country must be reverenced and obeyed and given way to even more than an angered father; that you must persuade it to the contrary or do what it bids and suffer quietly what it prescribes, whether blows or bonds, whether you are led to war for wounds or death, still, these things are to be done. The just lies here: never to give way, never to desert, never to leave your post, but in war or court of
c   law or any other place, to do what City and Country command—that, or to persuade it of what is by nature just. It is not holy to use force against a mother or father; and it is far more unholy to use force against your Country than against them."

What are we to say to that, Crito? Do the Laws speak the truth?

C. Yes, I think they do.

S. "Then consider this, Socrates," the Laws perhaps may say. "If we speak the truth, aren't you attempting to wrong us in what you now undertake? We gave you birth. We nurtured
d   you. We educated you. We gave to you and to every other

citizen a share of every excellence we could. Nonetheless, we continue to proclaim, by giving leave to any Athenian who wishes, that when he had been admitted to the rights of manhood and sees things in the City and its Laws which do not please him, he may take what is his and go either to one of our colonies or a foreign land. No law among us stands in the way or forbids it. You may take what is yours and go where you like, if we and the City do not please you.

e   But whoever among you stays, recognizing the ways we render judgment and govern the other affairs of the City, to him at that point we say that by his action he has entered agreement with us to do as we bid. And if he does not obey, we say that he commits injustice in three ways: because he disobeys us, and we gave him birth; because he disobeys us, and we nurtured him; because he agreed to obey us and

52a   neither obeys nor persuades us that we are doing something incorrect—even though we did not rudely command him to do as we bid, but rather set before him the alternatives of doing it or persuading us to the contrary. Those are the charges, Socrates, which we say will be imputable to you if you do what you're planning. To you, and to you not least, but more than any other Athenian.

And if I were to ask, "Why is that?", they might justly assail me with the claim that, as it happened, I more than most Athenians had ratified this agreement. They might

b   say, "Socrates, we have ample indication that we and the City pleased you. Otherwise, you wouldn't have stayed home in it to a degree surpassing all other Athenians. You never left to go on a festival, except once to the Isthmian Games. You never went anywhere else except on military service. You never journeyed abroad as other men do, nor had you any desire to gain knowledge of other cities and their laws—we and this our City sufficed for you. So eagerly did you choose us, so eagerly did you agree to live as a citi-

c   zen under us, that you founded a family here. That's how pleasing the City was to you. Even at your very trial, you could have proposed exile as a penalty, and done with the City's knowledge and permission what you're now attempting to do against her will. But at the time, you made a fine pretence of not being distressed at having to die. You'd choose death before exile—so you said. But now you feel no shame

at those words, nor any concern for we who are the Laws.
d   You attempt to destroy us by trying to run off like the
meanest of slaves, contrary to the compacts and agreements
you entered with us to live as a citizen. First of all, then,
tell us this: do we or do we not speak the truth when we
say that by your actions, if not your words, you have agreed
to live as a citizen under us?"

What am I to say to that, Crito? Must I not agree?

C. Necessarily, Socrates.

S. "Very well then," they might say. Aren't you trespassing
e   against your compacts and agreements with us? You didn't
agree under constraint, you weren't misled or deceived, nor
were you forced to decide in too little time. You had seventy years, during which time you could have gone abroad
if we did not please you, or your agreement came to seem
to you unjust. But you preferred neither Sparta nor Crete,
which you often used to say were well-governed, or any
53a   other City, Greek or barbarian. Quite the contrary: you
traveled abroad less often than the halt, the lame, and the
blind. So the City pleased you, to a degree surpassing all
other Athenians. Therefore, we pleased you, too, for to
whom would a city be pleasing without laws? Are you,
then, now not to abide by your agreements? If you are persuaded by us, Socrates, you will. You will not make yourself a butt of mockery by escaping.

"Consider too what good you will accomplish for yourself or your friends if you transgress or offend in this way.
b   That your friends risk prosecution themselves, with depri-
vation of city and confiscation of estate, could hardly be
more clear. But you first. If you were to go to any of the
cities nearest Athens, Thebes, say, or Megara, for both are
well-governed, you would go as an enemy to their polity.
Those concerned for their own cities would eye you with
suspicious, believing you to be a corrupter of laws. Again,
c   you would confirm the opinion of your judges and lead
them to think they rendered judgment justly, for a corrupter of laws may surely also be thought, and emphatically, a corrupter of young and ignorant men. Will you then
shun well-governed cities, and men of the more estimable
sort? What will life be worth to you if you do? Or will you
associate with them and without sense of shame discuss—

What will you discuss, Socrates? What arguments? The ones you used to offer here, about how virtue and justice are of highest worth for men, along with prescriptive custom and the Laws? 'The affair of Socrates'—don't you think it will look indecent? Surely you must. Then will you leave such places and go to Thessaly among Crito's friends? They're full of license and unchastened disorder in Thessaly, and no doubt they'd delight in hearing you tell your absurd story about how you ran off from prison dressed up in disguise—a peasant's leather coat, perhaps? Disguised like a runaway slave, just to change your looks! That you are an old man with probably only a little time to live, and yet cling boldly to life with such greedy desire that you will transgress the highest laws—will there be no one to say it? Perhaps not, if you give no offense. But otherwise, Socrates, you will hear many a contemptible thing said of yourself. Will you then live like a slave, fawning on every man you meet? And what will you do in Thessaly when you get there, besides eat, as if you'd exiled yourself for a banquet.[3] But as for those arguments of yours about justice and the other virtues—what will they mean to us then?

"Still, you want to live for your childrens' sake, so you can raise and educate them. Really? Will you take them to Thessaly and make foreigners out of them so they can enjoy that advantage too? If you don't, will they be better reared for your being alive but not with them? Your friends will look after them. Will they look after them if you go to Thessaly, but not if you go to the Place of the Dead? If those who call themselves your friends are really worth anything, you cannot believe that.

"Socrates, be persuaded by us, for we nurtured you. Put not life nor children nor anything else ahead of what is just, so that when you come to the Place of the Dead you may have all this to say in your defense to those who rule there. It will not appear better here, more virtuous, more just, more holy, for you or any of those around you to do this kind of thing here. And it will not *be* better for you on your arrival there. You now depart, if you depart, the victim of injustice at the hands of men, not at the hands of we who are the Laws. But if you escape, if you thus shamefully return injustice for injustice and injury for injury, if you trespass against your compacts and agreements with us, and work evil on those you least ought—yourself, your friends, your Country and its laws—we shall be angered at you while you live, and those our brothers who are the Laws in the Place of the Dead will not receive you kindly, knowing that you undertook so far as in you lay to destroy

d   us. Do not be persuaded to do what Crito bids. Be persuaded by us."

Crito, my dear and faithful friend, I think I hear these things as the Corybants think they hear the pipes, and the droning murmur of the words sounds within me and makes me incapable of hearing aught else. Be assured that if you speak against the things I now think true, you will speak in vain. Still, if you suppose you can accomplish anything, please speak.

C. Socrates, I cannot speak.

e   S. Very well, Crito. Let us so act, since so the God leads.

Notes and Selected Bibliography

Notes

PREFACE

1. It has been supposed that *Crito* 45b and 52c refer to *Apology* 37c-e, but they may equally refer to Socrates' actual words at the trial.

2. Printed in *Is Law Dead?*, ed. Rostow (New York, 1971), pp. 39–93.

IRONY AND RHETORIC

1. *D. L.* II. 40, trans. Hicks. The indictment is preserved with minor verbal difference in Xenophon's *Memorabilia* I. i.

2. Libanius wrote, not only an *Apologia Socratis*, but a declamation, *de Silentio Socratis*.

3. Dodds, *Plato's Gorgias* (Oxford, 1959), p. 370.

4. Ridell, *Plato's Apology* (Oxford, 1877), p. xxi, cited by Burnet, *Plato's Euthyphro, Apology, and Crito* (Oxford, 1924), p. 66.

5. Burnet, p. 67.

6. R. Hackforth (*The Composition of Plato's Apology* [Cambridge, 1933], pp. 55–57) denied the presence of rhetoric, parody, or irony in the exordium, on the ground that Socrates is simply telling the truth, that his points are natural, and his tone sincere. But Socrates can and does give a speech; that speech, both in style and structure, is a model of rhetorical art; and it is far from his accustomed manner of speaking—though not from his accustomed manner of reasoning. Anyone who doubts the presence of rhetoric may be asked to read the first page of the *Apology* aloud.

7. Dyer and Seymour, *Plato: Apology and Crito* (New York, 1949), p. 27.

8. See G. Norlin, *Isocrates* (Loeb), 2:182, cf. 1:xxvi., and R. J. Bonner, "The Legal Setting of Isocrates' *Antidosis*," *Classical Philology* 15 (1920):193. See also Bonner's, "The Legal Setting of Plato's *Apology*," *Classical Philology* (1908):168 ff.

9. See K. Dover, *Aristophanes: Clouds* (Oxford, 1968), p. xxvii.

10. *Rhetoric* II 1377b 32 ff., Oxford trans.

11. Compare *Gorgias* 452e ff. (and Aristotle *Rhetoric* I 1355b 26) with *Apology* 38d-e.

12. Hackforth, pp. 13-15, held that Xenophon could not have known Plato's *Apology* when he wrote his own, for if he had, he could not have supposed that the 'loftiness' had been left unexplained, nor have failed to recognize the superiority of Plato's account to his own. Waiving the fact that multiplying probabilities diminishes probability, and that the probabilities here are very slight, I respectfully suggest that Hackforth failed to see what Xenophon saw. Plato's *Apology* raises the direct question, Why was the defense so conducted that it almost necessarily failed? Xenophon's *Apology* attempts to offer a solution; it is irrelevant that the true solution lay elsewhere.

13. Paras. 1-5. Plato, *Apology* 40a-b, makes Socrates invoke the Sign because it did not *oppose* any of his actions, a fact which is taken to indicate that death is not an evil. By Plato's account, the Sign only prevented Socrates from doing things he is about to do. For Xenophon, the Sign advised Socrates what to do, and even offered free advice to friends.

HISTORICAL BACKGROUND OF THE CHARGES

1. Plutarch, *Pericles*, 32. But Plutarch also says that Pericles, fearing for Anaxagoras, sent him away from the city. If so, there was no trial, at least at this time.

2. Fr. 14 (Burtt).

3. *In Timarchum* 173.

4. The Thirty came to power in 404 B.C., after a reaction at the end of the Peloponnesian War, which the radical democracy was widely blamed for losing. Welcomed at first, the result was a reign of terror which lasted until, some eight months later, the oligarchy was overthrown. Critias and Charmides were not only once members of the Socratic circle, but also Plato's own kinsmen, whose judgment of them may be inferred from *Epistle* VII 324b-325a.

5. Paras. 5-6, trans. Van Hook. Diogenes Laertius (II. 38) records a tradition that Polycrates wrote Meletus' actual speech of accusation. But the tradition derives from Hermippus, an untrustworthy source, and Diogenes is hesitant about it; he goes on to say (II. 39), on the authority of Favorinus, scholar and friend of Plutarch, that Polycrates' speech mentioned the rebuilding of the long walls under Conon. Since the time of Bentley this account has been accepted, partly because Diogenes hesitates over Hermippus, partly because Favorinus is known on other grounds to be a reliable source.

Some students have attempted to date Plato's *Apology* by reading it as a reply to Polycrates; if that were so, the *Apology* must have been written around 390. But in fact, this conjecture is no more probable than that Polycrates wrote in reply to the *Apology*, or that Plato and Polycrates write quite independently of each other. Plato did not need the stimulus of a third-rate sophist to produce a masterpiece of art. It may be observed that here, as elsewhere, one must beware of the scholarly fallacy involved in supposing that multiplying probabilities increases probability.

6. Cf. Xenophan, *Memorabilia* I. ii. 12.

7. The case of Leon of Salamis was a precipitating cause of the overthrow of the Thirty.

8. Though one with a mixed reputation. Aristotle, in the *Constitution of Athens* (27.5) criticizes Pericles' institution of jury pay as leading to a deterioration in the quality of men who served, and goes on to remark, almost casually, "Moreover, bribery came into existence after this, the first person to introduce it being Anytus, after his command at Pylos [in 411 B.C.]. He was prosecuted by certain individuals on account of his loss at Pylos, but escaped by bribing the jury." In light of this and other evidence, it is not surprising that Plato so frequently describes the accusers of Socrates as knaves; cf. *Apology* 35d, 39a, 30c-d; *Gorgias* 521c-d. Diogenes Laertius (II. 63) says the Athenians, through remorse, exiled Any-

tus and Lycon and put Meletus to death. This is not dispositive evidence, but there is indication in the *Antidosis* (18–20) that Socrates' accusers may have suffered for their parts in the trial.

9. Xenophan, *Memorabilia* I. i. 9, trans. Marchant. Cobet suggested that the "accuser" is not Meletus but Polycrates. Polycrates' speech may well have been Xenophan's source, but it is hard to believe that Meletus did not argue according to this pattern: Xenophan himself supposed it.

LEGALITY

1. N. G. L. Hammond, *History of Greece* (London, 1967), p. 449, following J. B. Bury, *History of Greece* (London, 1903), p. 681. But see *Apology* 35c-d, 40a, *Crito*, 54b-c, *Gorgias* 486a, 521b-d.

2. *Apology* 37a-b. In the *Laws* (VI 766d-e) Plato rejects large juries on principle, and remarks of trials: "The matter in dispute on either side must always be made clear, and for elucidating the point at issue, lapse of time, deliberation, and frequent questionings are of advantage" (trans. Bury). He then goes on to provide for procedures which amount to appeal.

3. *The Wasps of Aristophanes* (London, 1915), pp. xxxvi-xxxviii.

4. Cf. *Crito* 45e, *Gorgias* 526e, and A. R. W. Harrison, *The Laws of Athens: Procedure* (Oxford, 1971), p. 156.

5. *Apology* 25d, cf. 27c. It will be observed that Socrates does not cross-examine Anytus and Lycon. It is unclear whether they were co-accusers (cf. *Apology* 23e, 36a), or principal witnesses who, as adverse, were treated as if they were accusers. The indictment is consistently treated as that of Meletus (*Euthyphro* 2b, 5a-b, 5c, 15e, *Apology* 24b ff.).

6. For an example, see *Apology* 19d.

7. *Apology* 34c-35a. Aristophanes satirizes the same thing in the *Wasps*, lines 568 ff., with deadly effect.

8. *Apology* 18d, and the frequent references to slander *passim*.

9. A prosecutor might be heard to say that a rich defendant should be convicted so that his estate might be confiscated, to the benefit of the citizenry. It is not by accident that Aristotle regards democracy as that form of government in which the poor rule and oppress the rich (*Politics* IV 1296a 27-32, cf. III 1279b 4-10, 15-26), and oligarchy as its opposite.

10. Harrison, *The Laws of Athens: Procedure*, p. 134.

11. Thus according to Herodotus (VI. xxi. 2), Phrynicus was fined a hundred drachmas in 493 B.C., "for having reminded the Athenians of their own misfortunes." And here is a client of Lysias, speaking a century later, about 395 B.C., a few years after the death of Socrates: "I have been trierarch five times, fought in four sea-battles, contributed to many war-levies, and performed my other liturgies as amply as any citizen. But my purpose in spending more than was enjoined upon me by the city was to raise myself the higher in your opinion, so that if any misfortune should befall me I might stand a better chance in court" (*Lysias* XXV 12–13, trans. Lamb, revised by J. K. Davies).

12. Aristotle, *Rhetoric* I 1375a 27-b17. This passage gives scant support for the peculiar thesis that the primary connotation of *nomos* from the end of the fifth century on is 'statute', a thesis, indeed, which must quite ignore the *Crito*.

13. *Thucydides* II. 37, trans. Jowett.

14. *Politics* III 1287a 28-32 (Welldon translation).

15. For the interview see (1609), 7 Co. *Rep.* 63-5.

16. Roscoe Pound, *An Introduction to the Philosophy of Law* (New Haven, 1954), p. 5.

17. Fuller, *The Morality of Law*, 2d ed. (New Haven, 1969), p. 91.

18. Hart, *The Concept of Law* (Oxford, 1961), p. 202.

HISTORICITY

1. Shorey, *What Plato Said* (Chicago, 1933), p. 81. To the contrary, see Burnet, pp. 63–68.
2. See also *Memorabilia* IV. viii.
3. *Phaedrus* 278e-279b.
4. [Plutarch], *Lives of the Ten Orators* 838F. Cf. Norlin, *Isocrates*, 1:xvii.
5. Norlin, *Isocrates*, 2:182.
6. Here are a few parallels, indicating the *Apology* by Stephanus page and the *Antidosis* by paragraph numbers in Norlin's edition: 15–19b; 18–35c-d; 21–37a-b; 26, 27–17d; 30–23c-d; 33, 34, 240–33d; 50–20d-e; 92–33a-b; 25, 301–36d; 99–33b; 100–34a; 177–32d; 179–17b; 241–34a-b; 272, 273–38c. This list does not pretend to be exhaustive.

THE APOLOGY

1. Meletus was quite young when he lodged his prosecution. See *Euthyphro* 2b.
2. A reference to Aristophanes, whose description of Socrates in the *Clouds* has in effect just been quoted, and who will later (19c) be mentioned by name.
3. Callias' answer is in the "short-answer" style of the Sophists. Cf. *Gorgias* 449b ff., *Protagoras* 334e-335c.
4. The leading democrats in Athens were forced into exile when the Thirty Tyrants came to power in 404 B.C.
5. The Priestess of Apollo, whose major shrine was Delphi.
6. A humorous oath. The Dog is the Egyptian dog-headed god, Anubis.
7. I.e., like Hercules.
8. The exact indictment is probably preserved in Diogenes Laertius II. 40; cf. Xenophon *Memorabilia* I. i. 1.
9. There is here, and throughout the following passage, a running pun on the name Meletus which cannot be preserved in translation: the name may mean 'he who exercises care or concern'.
10. Anaxagoras, a friend of Pericles, had also been indicted for impiety, and driven from the city.
11. A part of the Agora, or marketplace.
12. Aesclepius, for example, son of Apollo and the nymph Coronis. Note that nymphs are themselves goddesses.
13. For example, Achilles, son of the nymph Thetis and Peleus, a mortal father; or Heracles, son of Zeus and Alcmene, a mortal mother.
14. Achilles.
15. This is not a wholly accurate quotation from the *Iliad*, but describes the scene at XVIII 94 ff.
16. All battles in which Socrates fought with conspicuous bravery. See *Symposium* 220d-221b, *Laches* 181b.
17. The suggestion is that Meletus lodged his accusation of acknowledging new (or strange) gods because of the Sign. Cf. *Euthyphro* 3b.
18. The Council of Five Hundred, composed of fifty members from each of the ten Tribes.
19. After the democratic reforms of Cleisthenes in the sixth century, the Tribes of Athens were not constituted by blood-groups, but by residence at the time of reform; membership in them thereafter became hereditary. They were the basis of civil administration: the nine Archons and their Secretary, the ten Generals, and the ten Prytanies of the Council were chosen by the Tribes.
20. The Prytanies were the presiding officers of the Council, the representatives of each Tribe serving as a body for the tenth part of the year. They determined, among other things,

what business was to be brought before the Assembly, and one of their number was chosen as Epistates, or President, with responsibility for putting issues to a vote or refusing to allow a vote. According to Xenophon, Socrates was President on this occasion. Cf. *Gorgias* 473e-474a.

21. Arginusae, in 406 B.C. The battle was won by the Athenians, whose general failed to gather up the dead for burial, or to rescue the living who clung floating to the wrecks. The generals' defense (only eight of them, to be accurate, were actually tried, two *in absentia*) was that the ships detached for this purpose were prevented by weather, while the main body of the fleet was pursuing the beaten enemy. But they were charged with dereliction of duty, and by illegal proceedings condemned to death. As with Admiral Byng, there is some indication that this was done 'to encourage the others', and there is evidence in later Athenian naval history that it had just that effect. But the main reason appears to have been a wave of superstitious terror at having left the dead unburied.

22. Alopece. A deme was roughly the equivalent of a township.

23. Who, like Plato, went on to write Socratic dialogues.

24. Granting that there were 500 judges, the vote must have been 280 to 220.

25. A provision meant to prevent barratry, especially at the hands of the sycophants, or informers. Socrates affects to believe, with precisely the *eironeia* that caused much of the prejudice against him, that if 280 votes were cast against him, and he had three accusers, one-third of the votes should be assigned to each accuser. A pretty piece of reasoning, no doubt, but one hardly calculated to assuage his judges under the circumstances.

26. Under Athenian law, the prosecutor proposed a penalty, and the convicted defendant a counterpenalty; the jury was required to choose between them without alteration. The usual practice was for a convicted person to propose a penalty as heavy as he could bear short of that which the prosecutor demanded, in hope that the jury might accept it.

27. Public subsistence in the Prytaneum was a great honor, traditionally given to Olympic victors in major events.

28. It took considerable means, then as now, to raise and train horses.

29. Police magistrates chosen by lot, and charged with oversight of imprisonment and executions.

30. That is, an *eiron*. 'Irony' was regarded as a defect of character, not a virtue, as Theophrastus' portrait in the *Characters* of the ironical man makes clear.

31. It is useless to try to give modern money equivalents, but the ultimate fine proposed is substantial: Aristotle gives one mina as the conventional ransom for a prisoner of war (*Nichomachean Ethics* V 1134b 21). Why did Socrates propose a fine at all, or accept his friends' offer of suretyship? See 29d-30b, 30d-e.

32. The precise meaning of this prophecy is unclear. Burnet, on 39c 8, said that, "it is the programme of the *viri Socratici*. Plato tried to carry it out by making the voice of Socrates live after death." But something more seems meant than this. See, perhaps, *Antidosis* 18-20, Diogenes Laertius II. 43.

33. This phrase was excluded by Schleiermacher, who has been followed by others. But the manuscript tradition is unanimous in the reading, which is supported by *Euthyphro* 3b, *Theaetetus* 151a, and [*Theages*] 128e.

34. Of Persia, a proverbial symbol of wealth and power.

35. Agamemnon.

ANALYSIS

1. The *Crito* itself apart, this is supported by Xenophon's *Apology*, 23, and Diogenes Laertius II. 60, III. 35. The unusual length of time which intervened between trial and execu-

tion (*Phaedo* 58a-c) allowed Socrates' friends ample time to arrange an escape if they wished. Can it be doubted that they wished?

2. See Hippocrates, *Regimen* IV. xci, xcii.

3. E. R. Dodds, *The Greeks and the Irrational* (Berkeley, 1951), pp. 17-18.

4. *Rhetoric* II 1384a 23-27, trans. Roberts.

5. *Nichomachean Ethics* IV 1128b 21-26, trans. Ross. By way of contrast, see *Apology* 28b.

6. *Gorgias* 483d-484a. This is the first actual use of the expression 'law of nature' in western literature, though it is anticipated (see n. 7) in the Melian Dialogue.

7. Thucydides V. cv.: "Of gods we believe, and of men we know, that by a necessity of nature [*physis*] they rule when they have the power. We neither made this law [*nomos*] nor were the first to use it when made; we found it in existence, and will leave it so for all time. We use it knowing that you and others, possessed of like power, would do the same." And so the whole adult male population of the island was slain, and the women and children sold into slavery.

8. *Rhetoric* II 1384a 26-27.

9. The theme that virtue is the health of the soul runs through the whole of Plato's work. See, e.g., *Republic* IV 444 and X 609 ff., *Sophist* 228, *Politicus* 296, *Laws* X 906a.

10. Quoted by Sidgwick, *The Methods of Ethics* (London, 1962), p. 120.

11. And when they do, sometimes with surprising results: thus in the *Republic* (VII 556a-b), Plato recommends that commercial contracts be unenforceable at law. The reason is that he realized that the institution of contract was essential to the expansion of commerce, and he distrusted commerce.

12. Kant, *Fundamental Principles of the Metaphysics of Morals* (Abbott trans., 6th ed.), pp. 40 and 39 n. 1.

13. Austin, *How To Do Things with Words*, pp. 9-10. Italics Austin's.

14. Sidgwick, III. vi. 9, cf. III. vii. 3.

15. We may recall that an important part of what is at issue between Socrates and Thrasymachus in the *Republic* (I 348c-349a) is precisely whether justice is good.

16. See, among many examples in the Synoptic Gospels, *Luke* 6:27-38.

17. See Holmes, *The Common Law* (Boston, 1963), p. 15, with citations. Gibbon remarks: "The insolvent debtor was either put to death, or sold in foreign slavery beyond the Tiber; but if several creditors were alike obstinate and unrelenting, they might legally dismember his body, and satiate their revenge by this horrid partition. The advocates of this terrible law have insisted that it must strongly operate in deterring idleness and fraud" (*Decline and Fall of the Roman Empire*, XLIV:iii). This has an interesting bearing on the pound of flesh in *The Merchant of Venice*. Shylock was a Jew. But Jews had not been seen in England since their expulsion under Edward I. The penalty Shylock demands is Roman in origin, and his speech is laced with legal terms of the Lombard bankers who replaced the Jews. See Pollock and Maitland, *History of English Law*, 2d ed. (Cambridge, 1908), 2:225 and n. 2.

18. It will be observed that the notion of retribution here under discussion is moral. There are attempts to identify retribution with the principle of legality, *nulla poena sine lege*; but surely *ex post facto* law has often been applied on retributive grounds (cf. Aristotle, *Rhetoric* I 1375a 5). Again, a finding of guilt neither fixes a measure of punishment nor a limitation on punishment; see Hall, *General Principles of Criminal Law*, 2d ed. (Indianapolis: 1960), pp. 296-304; Gardner, "The Purposes of Criminal Punishment," *Modern Law Review* 21:117 ff.

19. *Deut.* 11:26. See also *Exod.* 21:23-35, *Lev.* 24:16-22. See also *Psalm* 137. One passage argues for the Talian Law as a thing to be justified apart from its divine warrant. That is

Deut. 19:18–21; the crime involved is abuse of judicial process by malicious accusation; and the reason given for applying the Talian Law is deterrence: "And those which remain shall hear, and fear, and shall henceforth commit no more evil among you." When pressed on a point which to them seems self-evident, the Furies give precisely the same justification in Aeschylus, *Eumenides*, lines 490–525.

20. In *Physics* 24.13 ff. (Diels), trans. Kirk and Raven.

21. *Gorgias* 478a ff., 525a-c, cf. *Sophist* 227b and Aristotle *Rhetoric* I 1369b 11-14: "To passion and anger are due all acts of revenge. Revenge and punishment are different things. Punishment is inflicted for the sake of the person punished; revenge for that of the punisher, to satisfy his feelings." Capital punishment, on this view, is appropriate in the case of incurables (whom Aristotle distinguished by their absence of remorse), on the ground that life is not worth living with a soul corrupted beyond cure. This view should be contrasted with another. In the nineteenth century, Sir James FitzJames Stephen remarked, among many notable sayings, that, "It is highly desirable that criminals should be hated, that the punishment should be so contrived as to give expression to that hatred, and to justify it . . . by gratifying an healthy natural sentiment"; and again, "The criminal law stands to the passion of revenge in much the same relation as marriage to the sexual appetite" (*History of the Criminal Law in England* [London, 1883], 2:83). This is an extreme form of the denunciatory theory of punishment, much in favor among British judges: the judge, in pronouncing sentence, expresses and ought to express the emotions of the community and their revulsion to the crime. This theory, as a theory, is unintelligible unless we trace it to its roots, which lie in Savigny and the school of historical jurisprudence: law is the natural and organic expression of 'the spirit of the people', a mystical entity, no doubt, but one which may be apprehended with clarity by jurists willing to abandon the superstition that to think is not less than to feel. The English have long prided themselves on their common sense; but it was an American, John Chipman Gray, who remarked that, "The *Volksgeist* carries a piece of sulphur in its waistcoat pocket to keep off rheumatism" (*The Nature and Sources of Law*). And it was a Greek, Aristotle, who said that law is reason without passion.

22. Thus Professor H. L. A. Hart (*Punishment and Responsibility* [Oxford, 1961], pp. 51–52), citing *Protagoras* 324 and *Laws* 861 and 865 for Plato's views on punishment, supposes that Plato's doctrines, if carried to their logical conclusion, would end in Erewhon, with punishment replaced by a system of 'social hygiene'. But the passages in the *Laws* do not deal with theory of punishment at all, but with issues involving what we should now call *mens rea*, and the *Protagoras* passage presents Protagoras' view, not Plato's. Plato believed that there is intrinsic moral benefit to the soul to be gained by punishment for wrongdoing, which is itself a symptom of disease of soul, and it is that benefit, not deterrence, which is the primary aim of punishment. Punishment, then, is not to be contrasted with or replaced by medicine, nor imposed so as to gain an opportunity to provide medicine. It *is* medicine. It may be added that as medicine is not prescribed in the absence of disease, so punishment is not prescribed in the absence of guilt.

23. *Nichomachean Ethics* I 1104b 13-18.

24. *Juris praecepta sunt haec: honeste vivere, alterum non laedere, suum cuique tribuere* (*Institutes* I. 3).

25. See Vinogradoff, *Outline of Historical Jurisprudence* (Oxford, 1922), 2:105 ff. See also H. L. A. Hart, *Definition and Theory in Jurisprudence* (Oxford, 1953), pp. 17-27. The *Interpretation Act*, 1889 (52 & 53 Vic. c. 63, sec. 2.19) defines 'person' to include 'body politic'.

26. Croiset, *Platon: Oeuvres Complètes* (Paris, 1966), 1:210 (Budé).

27. The analysis of law, Athenian or modern, involves more than courts: it involves agencies of legislation and administration as well. To say that any given principle is funda-

mental to a legal system is not to suggest that there are not other principles, logically independent of the first, which are equally fundamental.

28. Later antiquity and the eighteenth century pictured Socrates as a kind of Stoic sage. Plato's own portrait is different. Socrates is not the noblest Roman of them all, but a passionate Greek. David's painting, "The Death of Socrates," nicely sums up what Socrates was not: he was not a man given to delivering deathbed harangues in a toga.

29. *Politics* VI 1322a 5-7, trans. Jowett.

·30. I decide to plant a tree for shade in my backyard. This must be morally wrong, since I cannot consistently will that everyone should plant a tree for shade in my backyard: the fact that it is mine implies the right to exclude others. So the maxim of my action becomes inconsistent when universalized: universalization implies that no backyard is mine, while the original maxim implied that at least one backyard was mine. Kant's own assumptions to the contrary, it is difficult to reconcile the categorical imperative with the institution of private property—*proprium*.

31. L. Beauchet, *Histoire due droit privé de la République Athénienne* (Paris, 1897), 4: 38-39.

32. *Ibid.*, 4:38; see also Paton, *Jurisprudence* (Oxford, 1960), pp. 397-98.

33. As was not the case in Athens: a writ of outrage (*hybris*) was available for mistreatment of slaves. Harrison, *Law of Athens: Family and Property*, p. 163 n. 3 and pp. 166-71.

34. *Ibid.*, pp. 70-76.

35. See M. P. Nilsson, *History of Greek Religion*, 2d ed. (Oxford, 1952), chap. 7.

36. *Menexenus* 238d, *Ath. Pol.* 57, and C. Hignett, *History of the Athenian Constitution* (Oxford, 1968), pp. 38-46.

37. *Politics* I 1253a 19 ff., trans. Jowett.

38. 51e-52a, cf. 51b-c. The reference is in part procedural. The *Laws* offered Socrates, as they would any other citizen, fair trial in open court, and in no way hindered him in making his defense.

39. Common law distinguishes two types of invalidity. A void contract is one in which no contract has been formed despite the intention of the parties. This is true, for example, if a contract is entered to effect a criminal purpose: you cannot sue your partner in highway robbery for your rightful share of the spoils. In general, a void contract is without legal effect. A voidable contract, on the other hand, has legal effect, in that one party is bound and the other is not. If your agreement was induced by my use of fraud, duress, or undue influence, you are not bound, but I am bound in the unlikely event that you wish to hold me to it, and the *jus 'tertii* is preserved.

The distinction between void and voidable contracts is not in Athenian law, and in the only direct discussion of contract in the *Laws*, the Athenian Stranger collapses them, along with frustration: "Touching agreements, whenever a man undertakes and fails to fulfill his agreement—unless it be such as is forbidden by the laws or by a decree, or one made under forcible and unjust compulsion, or when a man is involuntarily prevented from fulfilling it owing to some unforeseen accident, actions may be brought before the tribal courts, if the parties are unable to come to a previous settlement before arbitrators or neighbors" (*Laws* XI 920d, trans. Bury).

40. Hyperbole for the sake of emphasis. As 51d makes clear, he was not legally capable of decision until admitted to the rights of manhood.

41. T. A. Sinclair, *History of Greek Political Thought* (London, 1959), p. 128, remarks, "How like Plato to forget that the vast majority of people have no freedom of choice as to where they live." In fact, it was not only possible but easy for Athenian citizens to emigrate, as Socrates himself suggests. Also, if the law does not forbid or penalize emigration, then

there is a right to emigrate. The motives among citizens for not exercising that right may be extremely various, and often compelling; but where the right exists, there is no legal coercion.

42. See Ernest Barker, *Greek Political Theory* (London, 1957), pp. 83–84, Guthrie, *A History of Greek Philosophy*, 3:107–12.

43. *Leviathan* I xiv 86–87 (Oakeshott).

44. Hall, *Studies in Jurisprudence and Criminal Theory* (New York, 1958), p. 50.

ASSUMPSIT

1. Pollock and Maitland, *History of English Law*, 2:212.

2. See *ibid.*, 2:526–27. The account here offered of Trespass, Case, and Assumpsit broadly follows that of Maitland in *The Forms of Action at Common Law* (Cambridge, 1965), Lecture VI. For bibliography on more recent work in what has become a much-disputed area, see S. F. C. Milsom's introduction to Pollock and Maitland, 2d ed., pp. lxxxix-xc.

3. "If a carpenter makes a covenant with me to make me a house good and strong and of a certain form, and he makes me a house which is weak and bad and of another form, I shall have an action of trespass on my case. So if a smith makes a covenant with me to shoe my horse well and properly, and if he shoes him and lames him, I shall have a good action. So if a doctor takes upon himself to cure me of disease, and he gives me medicines, but does not cure me, I shall have action on my case. . . . And the cause is in all these cases that there is an undertaking and a matter of fact beyond the matter which sounds merely in covenant. . . . In these cases the plaintiffs have suffered a wrong" (*per* Newton, J., Y.B. 14 Henry VI p. 18 [1436]), cited and translated by Holdsworth, *History of English Law* (London, 1942), 3:430.

4. Milsom, *Historical Foundations of the Common Law*, p. 273.

LEGAL OBLIGATION

1. Hart, *The Concept of Law*, p. 6.

2. Austin, *The Province of Jurisprudence Determined* (London, 1954), Lecture I.

3. It is interesting to compare Kelsen's induction: "What could the so-called law of ancient Babylonians have in common with the law that prevails today in the United States? What could the social order of a negro tribe under the leadership of a despotic chieftain—an order likewise called 'law'—have in common with the constitution of the Swiss Republic? Yet there is a common element, that fully justifies this terminology, and enables the word 'law' to appear as the expression of a concept with a highly significant social meaning. For the word refers to that specific social technique of a coercive order which . . . is yet essentially the same for all these peoples differing so much in time, in place, and in culture: the social technique which consists in bringing about the desired social conduct of men through the threat of a measure of coercion which is to be applied in the case of contrary conduct" (*General Theory of Law and the State* [New York, 1961], p. 19). And so, on the basis of this claim of fact, we reach a conclusion which concerns essence: "Law is the primary norm which stipulates the sanction."

4. *Rhetoric* I 1373b 3–11, trans. Roberts.

5. von Arnim, *Stoicorum Veterum Fragmenta* (Berlin, 1921), 2:1003, 3:314.

6. Cicero, *de Legibus* II. iv.

7. Blackstone, *Commentaries on the Laws of England* (San Francisco, 1890), p. 41; cf. p. 44.

8. See Aristotle, *Rhetoric* I xv.

9. Cf. Xenophon *Memorabilia* I. i. 18, and IV. iv. 2, and *Gorgias* 473-474a. The *Apology*

does not mention this fact, and Burnet on 32b 6 doubts its truth; but it is difficult to make sense of the outcry against Socrates except on this assumption, unless, as is unlikely, he had veto power as a mere member of the Prytanate.

10. *Rhetoric* I xv.

11. See C. K. Allen, *Law in the Making*, 7th ed. (Oxford, 1964), pp. 574, 582.

12. *Shaw v. D.P.P.* [1962], A.C. 220. House of Lords.

13. Gray, *The Nature and Sources of Law*, 2d ed. (Boston, 1962), p. 13.

14. See Hart, *The Concept of Law*, pp. 80–83.

15. One might imagine a transfer theory: if I am under obligation to obey the law, and the law requires of me what is unjust, it follows, not that I ought to do what I ought not do, but that I ought to do what the law ought not have obligated me to do. The responsibility for the wrong lies with the law, not with the agent bound to act according to it. This is the I-was-only-following-orders theory of jurisprudence, more often stated as a defense than defended. If X ought not be done, I ought not do it. A theory which maintains that I am under an obligation to do what ought not be done reduces to the theory that I ought to do what I ought not do. It reduces, that is, to the absurdity of (iii).

16. Compare the conclusion reached by an eighteenth-century New Jersey tailor, John Woolman: "I replied that in making covenants it was agreeable to honesty and uprightness to take care that we do not foreclose ourselves from adhering strictly to true virtue in all occurrences relating thereto. But if I should unwarily promise to obey the orders of a certain man, or number of men, without any proviso, and he or they command me to assist in doing some great wickedness, I may then see my error in making such a promise, and an active obedience in that case would be adding one evil to another. That though by such promise I shall be liable to punishment for disobedience, yet to suffer rather than to act appears to me more virtuous" (*The Journal* [Chicago, 1950], p. 75). It will be observed that Woolman supposes that the promise as such produces a moral claim even when it must be ignored; given the Socratic qualification, it does not.

17. The doctrine, that is, that no disobedience to the sovereign is justified, in any circumstances. For Macaulay's excellent discussion of this, see *History of England*, chap. 11.

THE CRITO

1. Who would be safe from the sycophants, or public informers, and the penalties of Athenian law.?

2. The word *musike* meant, not merely music, but any art over which the muses preside, and especially, in the education of children, poetry and literature. The word *gymnastike* had a similar breadth of meaning: it involved not only training in the skills of sport and war but in proper care of the body.

3. "The semi-barbarous hospitality of the Thessalian chiefs was notorious" (Burnet).

Selected Bibliography

Adam, J. *Platonis Crito*. Cambridge, 1890.

Adkins, A. W. H. *Merit and Responsibility*. Oxford, 1960.

Allen, C. K. *Law in the Making*. 7th ed. Oxford, 1964.

von Arnim, *H. Stoicorum Veterum Fragmenta*. Vol. 2. Berlin, 1921.

Austin, J. *The Province of Jurisprudence Determined*. Edited by H. L. A. Hart. London, 1954.

Beauchet, L. *Histoire due droit privé de la République Athénienne*. Paris, 1897.

Blackstone, W. *Commentaries on the Laws of England*. 8th ed. Edited by Hammond. San Francisco, 1890.

Bonner, R. J., and Smith, G. *The Administration of Justice from Homer to Aristotle*. Chicago, 1930, 1938.

Buckland, W. W. *A Manual of Roman Private Law*. Cambridge, 1925.

Burnet, J. *Plato's Euthyphro, Apology, and Crito*. Oxford, 1924.

——. *Essays and Addresses*. New York, 1930.

Calhoun, G. M. *The Growth of Criminal Law in Ancient Greece*. Berkeley, 1927.

Calogero, G. *Il Critone*. Firenze, 1959.

Croiset, M. *Platon: Oeuvres Complètes*. Vol. 1. Edited by Budé. Paris, 1966.

Davies, J. K. *Athenian Propertied Families: 600-300 B.C.* Oxford, 1971.

Dodds, E. R. *Plato's Gorgias*. Oxford, 1959.

——. *The Greeks and the Irrational*. Berkeley, 1951.

Dover, K. *Aristophanes: Clouds*. Oxford, 1968.

Dyer, L., and Seymour, T. D. *Plato: Apology and Crito*. New York, 1908.

Fleming, J. G. *Introduction to the Law of Torts*. Oxford, 1967.

Fuller, Lon. *The Morality of Law*. 2d ed. New Haven, 1969.

Gray, J. C. *The Nature and Sources of Law*. 2d ed. Boston, 1962.

Guthrie, W. K. C. *A History of Greek Philosophy: III. The Fifth Century Enlightenment*. Cambridge, 1968.

Hackforth, R. *The Composition of Plato's Apology*. Cambridge, 1933.

Hall, J. *General Principles of Criminal Law*. 2d ed. Indianapolis, 1960.

——. *Studies in Jurisprudence and Criminal Theory*. New York, 1958.

Hammond, N. G. W. *History of Greece*. London, 1967.

Harrison, A. R. W. *The Law of Athens*. Vol. 1, *Family and Property*. Oxford, 1968; vol. 2, *Procedure*, 1971.

Hart, H. L. A. *The Concept of Law*. Oxford, 1961.

——. *Definition and Theory in Jurisprudence*. Oxford, 1953.

——. *Punishment and Responsibility*. Oxford, 1968.

Hignett, C. *History of the Athenian Constitution*. Oxford, 1968.

Holdsworth, W. *History of English Law*. Vol. 3. 5th ed. London, 1942.

Holmes, O. W., Jr. *The Common Law*. Edited by Howe. Boston, 1963.

Jones, A. H. *Athenian Democracy*. London, 1960.

Jones, J. W. *Law and Legal Theory of the Greeks*. Oxford, 1956.

Kelsen, H. *General Theory of Law and the State*. New York, 1961.

Maitland, F. W. *The Forms of Action at Common Law*. Edited by Chaytor and Whittaker. Cambridge, 1965.

Maitland, F. W., and Pollock, F. *History of English Law*. 2d ed. Edited by Milsom. Cambridge, 1968.

Milsom, S. F. C. *Historical Foundations of the Common Law*. London, 1969.

Pound, R. *An Introduction to the Philosophy of Law*. New Haven, 1954.

Ridell, W. *Plato's Apology*. Oxford, 1877.

Rostow, E. V. *Is Law Dead?* New York, 1971.

Saunders, T. J. *Plato: The Laws*. London, 1970.

Sinclair, T. A. *History of Greek Political Thought*. London, 1959.

Sidgwick, H. *The Methods of Ethics*. 7th ed. London, 1962.

Shorey, P. *What Plato Said*. Chicago, 1933.

Sohm, R. *The Institutes of Roman Law*. Oxford, 1907.

Taylor, A. E. *Plato*. 4th ed. New York, 1950.

Vinogradoff, P. *Outlines of Historical Jurisprudence*. Vol. 2. Oxford, 1922.

West, T. G. *Plato's Apology of Socrates*. Ithaca, 1979.

Woolman, John. *The Journal*. Edited by J. Whitney. Chicago, 1950.

Woozley, A. D. *Law and Obedience: The Arguments of Plato's Crito*. London, 1979.

Indices

Index of Passages Cited

145

Index of Names

Aeschines, 5, 18
Alcibiades, 19, 34
Anaxagoras, 18
Anytus, 6, 14, 19, 20, 44
Arginusae, 53, 104
Aristophanes, 19, 39
Aristotle, 28, 30, 68, 70, 89, 103
Austin, J. L., 73
Austin, John, 100, 104, 107, 108, 109

Bentham, Jeremy, 26, 106
Blackstone, William, 27, 103, 107
Burnet, John, 5

Callicles, 4, 11, 70, 91, 92
Charmides, 19
Clarke, Samuel (Boyle Lectures), 71
Critias, 19

Diogenes Laertius, 3
Dodds, E. R., 5
Dyer, L., 6

Eleatic Stranger, 12

Fuller, Lon, 32

Glaucon, 91, 92
Gray, John Chipman, 108

Hall, Jerome, 95
Harrison, A. R. W., 26
Hart, H. L. A., 32, 100
Hesiod, 18
Hobbes, Thomas, 94, 100
Homer, 18
Hume, David, 112

Isocrates, 5, 19, 34, 35

Kant, Immanuel, 72, 73
King Archon, 23

Laws of Athens, 17, 81 ff.
Leon of Salamis, 53
Libanius, 4
Lycon, 6, 14, 19, 44
Lysias, 5, 26

Madison, James, 31
Maitland, F. W., 97
Meletus, 3, 6, 7, 9, 14, 15, 18, 19, 20, 25, 44
Milsom, S. F. C., 99